**AMERICAN SCHOOL OF
NEEDLEWORK**

PRESENTS

The Great CRAFT-QUILTS Book

President: Jean Leinhauser
Vice President and Book Coordinator: Rita Weiss
Project Coordinators: Meredith Montross and Jane Meyers
Art Director: Carol Wilson Mansfield

Photography by Stemo Photography, Inc., Northbrook, Illinois
Roderick A. Stemo, President
James E. Zorn, Photographer

Book Design by CBG Graphics, Hartsdale, New York
Carol Belanger Grafton, Designer

STERLING PUBLISHING CO., NEW YORK

FOREWORD

I am sure that there are people who strongly believe that they are the originators of the "craft quilt", but let me assure you that no one enjoys making them more than we here at the American School of Needlework do.

It all began when we started our quilting department. Our offices became filled with the most beautiful traditional patchwork and appliqué quilts. Soon our other departments decided to try and see if they couldn't apply their talents to making quilts. One day our cross stitchers dreamed up a cross-stitch quilt, and before we realized what had happened each department was busily making a quilt—using its own particular skills. Our art department designed painted quilts; our embroiderers produced embroidered quilts, and our stencilers appeared with a pair of beautifully stenciled quilts.

And so the "craft quilt" was born.

In this book we share some of our "craft quilts" with you. You don't have to be a proficient quilt maker to produce a

beautiful "craft quilt". Just apply your favorite craft and proceed to create a quilt. If you like to cross stitch, try our "Sunbonnet Sue Cross-Stitch Quilt"; if you enjoy painting, why not make a delightful painted teddy bear quilt. If you enjoy sewing on the sewing machine, try making a quilt entirely on the sewing machine.

If you haven't mastered any particular craft, we've included step-by-step instructions on working each skill. We invite you to learn a new craft and then to make use of it to produce a magnificent "craft quilt". I know you will enjoy "craft quilting" as much as we.

Jean Leinhauser

Jean Leinhauser, *President*
American School of Needlework, Inc.
P.O. Box 1183, Northbrook, Illinois
60062

ACKNOWLEDGMENTS

To ensure the accuracy and clarity of our instructions, all of the projects in this book were tested by a group of dedicated and hard-working women, who made the designs which we have photographed. We express our appreciation to the following group of pattern testers:

Ruth Adair, Beverly Cartwright, Almeda Colby, Jan Corbally, Judy Demain, Pat Edwalds, Marilyn Hooper, Barbara Hunter, Rosemary Joseph, Marilyn Kleinhardt, June Krenzel, Jean Leinhauser, Joyce Lerner, Carol Wilson Mansfield, Betsy Meyers, Jane Meyers, Andrea Montross, Meredith Montross, Patricia Rankin, Martha Scott, Judy Shambrook, Bea Slattery, Addie Snett, Rosemarie Stanley, Pat Steiner, Steffi Sullivan, Shirley Sutschek, Phyllis Sylvester, Sue Todd, Mary Ellen Wyld, Ame Zarski and Charlotte Zarski.

We also acknowledge our thanks and appreciation to the following group of contributing designers:

Louise O'Donnell, Carol Wilson Mansfield, Jane Meyers and Rita Weiss.

Copyright © 1984 by the American School of Needlework, Inc.
Published by Sterling Publishing Co., Inc.
Two Park Avenue, New York, N.Y. 10016

Available in Canada from Oak Tree Press, Ltd.
℅ Canadian Manda Group, P.O. Box 920, Station U,
Toronto, Ontario M8Z 5P9

Manufactured in the United States of America
All rights reserved
Sterling ISBN 0-8069-5538-4

Contents

General Directions

Before starting to work on your craft-quilt, read through these general directions on making a quilt. Most of the quilts in this book are made in this manner with individual blocks, framing, sashing, borders and binding. A few of the quilts do not have framing, and the sewing machine quilts have no framing or sashing. Look at *Fig 1* which explains the different parts of a quilt.

A ¼" seam allowance—which is standard in quilt making—is used for all quilts. Seams in quilt making are pressed flat to one side, not open. Open seams will weaken the quilt. Generally seams can all be pressed in the same direction, but darker pieces should not be pressed so that they fall under lighter pieces since they may show through when the quilt is completed. If you turn seams on the top in one direction and seams on the bottom in the other, you will keep seams that are crossed from bunching at crossing points (*Fig 2*). Clip away excess fabric if necessary. All seams should be ironed before they are crossed with another seam.

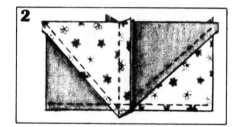

CHOOSING THE FABRIC

The best fabric for quilt making is 100% cotton. If you have difficulty locating 100% cotton, you can use a blend, but try not to use anything with more than approximately 30% synthetic.

Unless you are told otherwise (as in Candlewicking) be sure to wash your fabric before you begin to work on your quilt. This will enable you to check that your fabric is colorfast and preshrunk (don't trust those manufacturers' labels). Test for colorfastness by washing in fairly hot water. Be especially wary of reds and dark blues; they have a tendency to bleed if the initial dyeing was not carefully done. Fabrics which continue to bleed after they have been washed several times should be eliminated.

Make sure your fabric is absolutely square. If it is not, you will have difficulty cutting square pieces. Fabric is woven with a crosswise and lengthwise thread. Lengthwise threads should be parallel to the selvage (that's the finished edge along the sides; sometimes the fabric company prints its name along the selvage), and crosswise threads should be perpendicular to the selvage (*Fig 3*). If fabric is off-grain, you can straighten it. Pull gently on the true bias in the opposite direction to off-grain edge (*Fig 4*). Continue doing this until crosswise threads are at a right angle to lengthwise threads.

1

block   block

sashing

binding

quilting   framing   border

backing

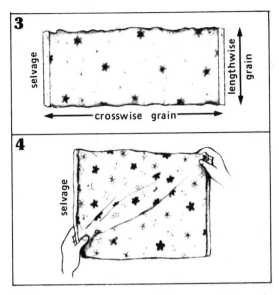

While we are talking about fabric, a word about thread. Regular sewing thread is used to join blocks. (The color does not have to match; just be sure it will not show through any of the pieces.) Don't use "quilting thread" for sewing blocks. Quilting thread is too thick, and your seams that cross will become too bulky. Quilting thread is used later for the actual quilting.

PREPARING THE BLOCKS

Instructions with each quilt will tell you how to prepare the quilt blocks for that quilt. Blocks are usually washed and steamed dry after they have been worked.

BLOCKING THE BLOCKS

Blocks will usually be prepared on a larger piece of fabric than the final size is to be. When blocks have been finished, washed and ironed, it is time to cut them to their final size and block them to a perfect square. An easy way to do this is to cut a cardboard square which is the size of the fabric you have been working on, with an opening cut in its center which is the size the finished block is to be. *Fig 5* shows a 14″ cardboard square with a 10½″ opening in preparation to cut a 10½″ block. This becomes a template for cutting blocks to right size. Place block face up on a hard surface. Place template over block, carefully centering it over design. With pencil, lightly mark around inner template opening, then cut block along these lines. Do this for each block. Place each cut block face down on ironing board, pull until it is exactly square, pin corners, and steam with damp cloth. Do not let iron rest on the stitches; let the steam do the work!

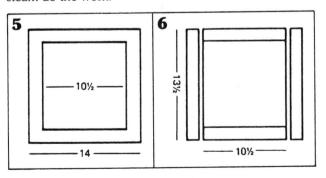

FRAMING THE BLOCKS

The four strips which surround the blocks are called "The Framing". Cut four framing strips for each block; the sizes will be given with each quilt.

Place one of the shorter strips across the side of a block, right sides together, and sew by hand or machine as shown in *Fig 6* stitching along the ¼″ seam. (Use this seam allowance throughout.) Place a second shorter strip across other side of a block and join in same manner. Then join two longer strips to top and bottom (*Fig 6*). Press all seams flat to one side, not open. Press away from block. Repeat for every block.

ADDING SASHING

Sashing is the term for the strips which are used between the blocks. Quilts with many different patterns in the blocks—such as most of the quilts shown here—always look better when set apart with strips. Instructions for cutting and sewing the sashing are given with each quilt. When the same quilt block is used—as in our sewing machine quilts—sashing is usually not necessary. In fact, the design of the completed quilt often is only apparent when the blocks are set with no division between them, creating optical illusions.

ADDING THE BORDERS

Just as most pictures look better framed, most quilts look best with borders. The instructions for cutting and sewing borders are given with each quilt. If you do not have enough fabric for the long strips, you can piece them. These pieced seams will be hardly noticeable in the finished quilt, but be sure to iron the seams before joining the strips.

PREPARING THE QUILT TOP

A completed quilt consists of three parts: top, filler or batting, and backing. Quilting stitches are used to hold the top to both backing and batting. If you don't want to quilt the top, you can tie it. This is a traditional method and quite satisfactory.

If you are going to quilt this project, you will need to mark the quilting pattern before joining it to batting and backing. If you are going to tie quilt, skip next section on marking quilting design.

MARKING THE QUILTING DESIGN: Most of the craft quilts pictured on this book have been quilted around the individual designs. Although this is not essential it does add dimension to your quilt. Quilting around the pattern pieces need not be marked on the quilt top. You merely quilt ¼″ around the pattern (or inside the seam line on the sewing machine quilts), and you can do this by eye. You may, however, wish to mark the quilting motif on sashing and borders. Suggestions for this design is given with each quilt in the construction diagram. *Fig 7* is our suggested quilting pattern for sashing and borders. If you wish to use this pattern, trace *Fig 7* onto heavy cardboard or plastic and carefully cut it out. This is your quilting template; use it to mark the quilting lines on the **right** side of fabric. For marking, use a hard lead pencil, chalk, or one of the special water-soluble marking pens. If you quilt right on marked lines, they will not show. Be sure to test any marking material to find one that works best for you.

7

QUILTING TEMPLATE

ATTACHING BATTING AND BACKING: There are a number of different types of batting on the market. Thin batting will require a great deal of quilting to hold it (quilting lines no more than 1″ apart); very thick batting can be used *only* for tied quilts. For a first quilting project, buy a medium weight bonded polyester sheet batting. You'll be able to do as much or as little quilting or tying as you wish without fear of batting slipping around when quilt is washed. Don't buy polyester *stuffing* which is intended for pillows or toys. Sheet batting is made especially for quilts; it is bonded into a flat sheet and then rolled for ease in handling.

Fabric for backing should be soft and loosely woven so that the quilting needle can pass through evenly. Bedsheets are usually not good backing material. Cut batting and backing approximately 2″ wider on all sides than quilt top. Place backing, wrong side up, on flat surface. Place batting on top of this, matching outer edges. Pin backing and batting together; then baste with long stitches, starting in center and sewing toward edges in a number of diagonal lines. Now center quilt top, right side up, on top of batting. Baste top to batting and backing layers in same manner.

QUILTING THE TOP

The actual quilting stitch is really a fairly simple one for anyone who has ever sewn. There are many books which attempt to teach the quilter how to make the proper stitch. It's something like teaching someone to swim with a swimming manual. You're never really going to learn unless you dive right into the water!

The stitch is just a very simple running stitch, but working through three layers at once may be a bit difficult at first. Instead of just horizontally pushing the needle through the fabric and then pulling it out in one motion, you will probably have to push it vertically all the way through the three layers on one side and then push it back in what amounts to two separate motions.

Use one of the short, fine needles especially designed for quilting (they are often called "betweens"), and 100% cotton quilting thread.

By the way, all quilters wear thimbles! If you have never used a thimble before, you are going to have to now. The thimble is worn on the middle finger of your right hand (or your left, if you are left-handed). The thimble is used to push the needle through the fabric as in **Fig 8**. The quilting can be done in a traditional floor frame, but chances are you'll probably find a quilting hoop more convenient. Place hoop over middle of the quilt, pull quilt slightly taut (not as stretched as for embroidery) and move extra fullness toward edges. Begin working in center and quilt toward outer edges. As you work, you will find the quilting stitch has a tendency to push batting, and by working from

center out you can gradually ease any excess fullness toward edges. If you wish, run quilting thread through beeswax to keep it from tangling.

8

Begin with an 18″ length of thread, with a knot in one end. Go into quilt through top about ½″ from where you plan to begin quilting, and bring needle up to quilting line. Pull gently but firmly, and knot will slip through into batting where it will disappear. Now place left hand under hoop where needle should come through. With right hand push needle vertically downward through layers of the quilt until it touches left hand.

If you are a beginning quilter, you may need to pull needle through with left hand, and push it back upward to where it is received by right hand, close to last stitch. As you become more proficient, you will be able to do the whole operation with one hand, merely using left hand to signal that needle has penetrated three layers. Some experienced quilters are able to put several stitches on the needle just as if they were sewing.

Make stitches as close together as you can; this is the real secret of beautiful quilting. The stitches should be evenly spaced, and same length on front as on back. When entire quilt has been quilted, lift it from frame or hoop and remove basting stitches. Proceed to section on Attaching the Binding.

TYING THE TOP

Use knitting worsted weight yarn (washable of course), crochet thread, several strands of embroidery floss or other washable material.

Work from center of the quilt out, adjusting any excess fullness of batting as you go. Thread an 18″ length of yarn into a large-eyed needle. Do not knot! Take needle down from top through all three layers, leaving about 1″ of yarn on right side. Bring needle back up from wrong side to right side, about ⅛″ from where needle first entered. Tie a firm knot, then cut, leaving both ends about ½″ long. Make sufficient ties to keep the three layers together.

ATTACHING THE BINDING

Place quilt on a flat surface and carefully trim backing and batting ½″ beyond quilt top edge. Measure quilt top and cut two 2″ binding strips from fabric listed for binding, the length of your quilt (for sides). Right sides together, sew one side strip to one side of quilt with ¼″ seam allowance (seam allowance should be measured from outer edge of quilt top fabric, not outer edge of batting/backing). Turn binding to back and turn under ¼″ on raw edge; slip stitch to backing. Do other side in same manner. Then carefully measure and cut two 2″ binding strips for top and bottom, and attach in same manner as sides.

Counted Cross Stitch

For many of us the words "cross stitch quilt" bring visions of working hundreds of boring blue crosses stamped on a large piece of fabric. Counted cross stitch, however, is not worked from a boring stamped design but by counting threads in the fabric and working from a chart. It's a lot of fun as you watch the design take shape on blank fabric.

COUNTED CROSS STITCH HOW-TO

THE FABRICS

Evenweave fabrics which are designed especially for embroidery and are woven with the same number of vertical and horizontal threads per inch are used for counted cross stitch. Cross stitches are made over the intersections of the horizontal and vertical threads, and because the number of threads in each direction is equal, each stitch will be the same size and perfectly square.

The fabrics most commonly used are Aida Cloth and Hardanger Cloth. Aida is a basketweave fabric in which horizontal and vertical threads are grouped, making the intersections for stitches very easy to see. Aida is woven with the intersections spaced in three different sizes: 11 count (11 stitches to the inch); 14 count (14 stitches to the inch) and 18 count (18 stitches to the inch). Hardanger is woven with pairs of vertical and horizontal threads; the intersections in Hardanger are visible but not as pronounced as in Aida. All Hardanger is 22 count fabric (22 stitches to the inch), but designs can be worked over two threads which will make the count 11 stitches to the inch.

HOOPS

Counted cross stitch can be done with or without a hoop. If you choose to stretch the fabric in a hoop, use one made of plastic or wood with a screw type tension adjuster. Placing a small hoop over existing stitches will slightly distort them but a gentle raking with the needle will restore their square shape.

NEEDLES

Cross stitch is done with a blunt-pointed tapestry needle. The needle slips between the threads, not through them. *Fig 1* will tell you which size needle is appropriate for each kind of fabric.

FLOSS

Any six-strand cotton embroidery floss can be used for cross stitch. The six-strand floss can be divided to work with one, two or three strands as required by the fabric. *Fig 1* tells how many floss strands to use with the various fabrics.

THE STITCHES

A single cross stitch is formed in two motions. Following the numbering in *Fig 2*, bring threaded needle up at 1, down at 2, up at 3, down at 4, completing the stitch.

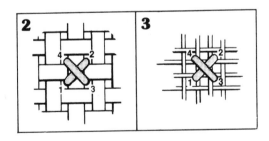

When working on Aida cloth, *Fig 2*, your stitch will cover one "block" of fabric. When embroidering on a more simply-woven fabric with stitches to be worked over two threads, *Fig 3*, make sure the first downward motion (2) is over an uppermost thread of the weave, to prevent the stitch from "disappearing" into the weave.

When working stitches over one thread or three threads, pull thread through fabric each time the needle is inserted (stab stitch method); do not "sew" the stitches as they tend to disappear in the weave. *NOTE: Hardanger fabric is described as having 22 threads per inch—it is actually 22 pairs of threads.*

1

FABRIC	STITCHES PER INCH	STRANDS OF FLOSS	TAPESTRY NEEDLE SIZE
Aida	11	3	24
Aida	14	2	24, 25 or 26
Aida	18	1 or 2	24, 25 or 26
Hardanger	22	1	24, 25 or 26

Work horizontal rows of stitches, *Fig 4*, whenever possible. Bring thread up at 1, holding tail end of thread beneath fabric and anchoring it with your first few stitches. Work half of each stitch across the row left-to-right; complete the stitches on the return journey.

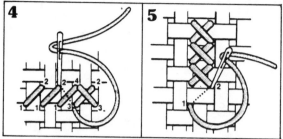

When a vertical row of stitches, *Fig 5*, is appropriate, complete each stitch then proceed to the next. End thread by weaving over and under several stitches on the wrong side of fabric; begin new threads in this manner if stitches are available.

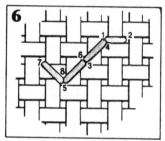

Back stitches are usually worked after cross stitches have been completed. They may slope in any direction and are occasionally worked over more than one fabric block or thread. *Fig 6* shows the progression of several stitches; bring thread up at odd numbers, down at even numbers.

THE CHARTS

Each square on a charted design equals the space occupied by one cross stitch. The symbol in a square represents the thread color to be used for that stitch. Dark lines indicate back stitches.

Each chart is accompanied by a stitching key showing:
- **a)** the symbol for each color (by DMC number and by name—you may substitute with a comparable brand of 6-strand floss, pearl cotton or yarn);
- **b)** back stitch and other special directions;

To determine the finished dimensions of a stitched area, multiply the number of stitches in the design's width by the number of stitches per inch of the fabric you select; repeat for height. For example, 11 stitches per inch are achieved by using Aida 11 or Hardanger—worked over 2 threads; 14 stitches per inch are achieved by using Aida 14 or Fiddler Cloth (14). Be sure to allow enough additional fabric for a pleasing border, plus whatever is required for finishing. Cut fabric along its weave. An overcast or machine zig-zag stitch around the raw edges will minimize raveling.

At the top and side of each chart are marks which indicate the center (which may be a row of stitches, or between two rows of stitches). Find the center of the fabric by folding it in half horizontally and then vertically. Baste along both fold lines; the basting (which is removed when stitching is complete) will cross at the middle and aid in counting stitches.

THE FINISHING

Dampen embroidery (or wash in mild soapsuds if soiled and rinse well); roll it in a clean towel to remove excess moisture. Place embroidery face down on a dry, clean terry towel and iron carefully until dry and smooth. Make sure all thread ends are well-anchored and clipped closely, then proceed with desired finishing.

When machine-stitching on evenweave fabric—whenever possible, place the layer of fabric that will become the front of the project uppermost under the presserfoot; stitch carefully, using either the fabric weave or a constant distance from the embroidery as your guideline.

CROSS STITCH SUNBONNET SUE CRIB QUILT

The perennial favorite, Sunbonnet Sue, appears here in an easy-to-make cross stitch quilt. The blocks can be worked over two threads of hardanger or, if you prefer, on 11-count Aida. First Sue plants her seeds, then she waters her garden, then she hoes her rows, and finally she has a beautiful flower to offer as a gift to the new baby.

Size

Approx 33″ × 47″

Materials and Equipment

All fabric requirements are based on 44″–45″ wide material. If you use narrower-width fabric, adjust yardage accordingly. (Try to get 100% cotton or a blend with no more than 30% synthetic.)

½ yd Hardanger (*for cross-stitch blocks*) or 11-count Aida cloth
1 yd solid fabric (*for sashing and borders*)
1 yd gingham fabric (*for binding and backing*)
1 package crib size quilt batting
6 strand embroidery floss

DMC
208 Purple	729 Gold
350 Coral	813 Light Blue
352 Light Coral	825 Blue
353 Pink	911 Green
434 Brown	954 Light Green

Fabric shears and embroidery scissors
Sewing, cross-stitch and quilting needles
Sewing and quilting thread (*white is preferred*) or yarn for tying
Standard quilting supplies

Before cutting, wash and iron fabrics to be used for sashing, borders, backing and binding. Make sure that the grain of all fabric is straight.

Instructions

Step 1: Cut a piece of cross-stitch fabric 8½″ × 10″ for each block. Cut all blocks before beginning stitching; make sure that they are all cut the same direction. Following instructions on pages 7-8, cross stitch the 12 blocks. Note that you work each design three times with three different color combinations. The stitch dimensions for each Sunbonnet Sue design is 43 high by 60 wide. Each design is worked in the border, which is shown once; the design position in the border is shown by dotted lines. Wash block as described on page 00. Carefully measuring from centers out, cut each block 7½″ wide by 8½″ high.

Step 2: There is no framing around the blocks in this quilt. From sashing fabric, cut nine sashing strips 3½″ wide × 7½″ long. Making sure top of each design is in right position, place first sashing strip (**Fig 1: No. 1**) across bottom of "Block A" right sides together and stitch. Then sew same piece of sashing to top of "Block D". In same manner stitch second sashing strip (**Fig 1: No. 2**) to bottom of "Block D" and then to top of "Block G". Join third sashing strip (**Fig 1: No. 3**) to bottom of "Block G" and to top of "Block J". You now have a vertical strip of four joined blocks. Following Fig 1 for placement, make two more vertical strips of four joined blocks. You now have three vertical strips each measuring about 41½″ (which includes ¼″ seam allowance at top and bottom). Press all seams to one side before joining next seam.

Step 3: Cut two sashing strips each 3½″ wide and 41½″ long (or length of your strip of blocks). Sew one strip to each side of center row of blocks (**Fig 1: Nos. 10 and 11**). Sew first and third row of blocks to these same strips, being sure that tops and bottoms of all blocks line up exactly. Press seams.

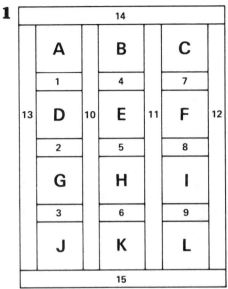

Step 4: Now complete quilt top by adding borders to top, bottom and sides. Cut four border strips, each 3½″ wide. Cut two 41½″ long (or length of your quilt top) and two 33½″ wide (or width of your quilt top). In same manner as for vertical sashing, sew two longer border strips to right and left sides of quilt top (**Fig 1: Nos. 12 and 13**). Then sew shorter border strips to top and bottom (**Fig 1: Nos. 14 and 15**). Give quilt top final steaming, making sure all corners are square and that all seams are pressed to one side.

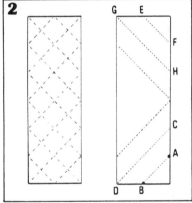

Step 5: Quilt or tie top and attach binding following directions on page 6. In the quilt shown in the photo, a 1″ binding is showing all around. Follow the directions on page 6, but cut your binding strip 2½″ wide and trim backing and batting ¾″ beyond quilt top edge. The quilting template can be used. To make the diamond shapes as in the photographed quilt, mark the quilt top as follows along the sashing and borders only. Begin in the lower right hand corner of the border and measure 2″ up from bottom (**Fig 2**). Make a small mark (A). Make another similar mark along the bottom of the border 2″ in from the right hand corner (B). Join these two marks with a diagonal line (AB). Starting at this bottom diagonal line, make diagonal lines 2″ apart (measuring from mark A) from the bottom right of the border to the top left (C-D, etc.) Using this same technique, draw intersecting diagonal lines across the border, from top right to the bottom left (E-F, etc.) The intersections will make the diamond shaped quilting design.

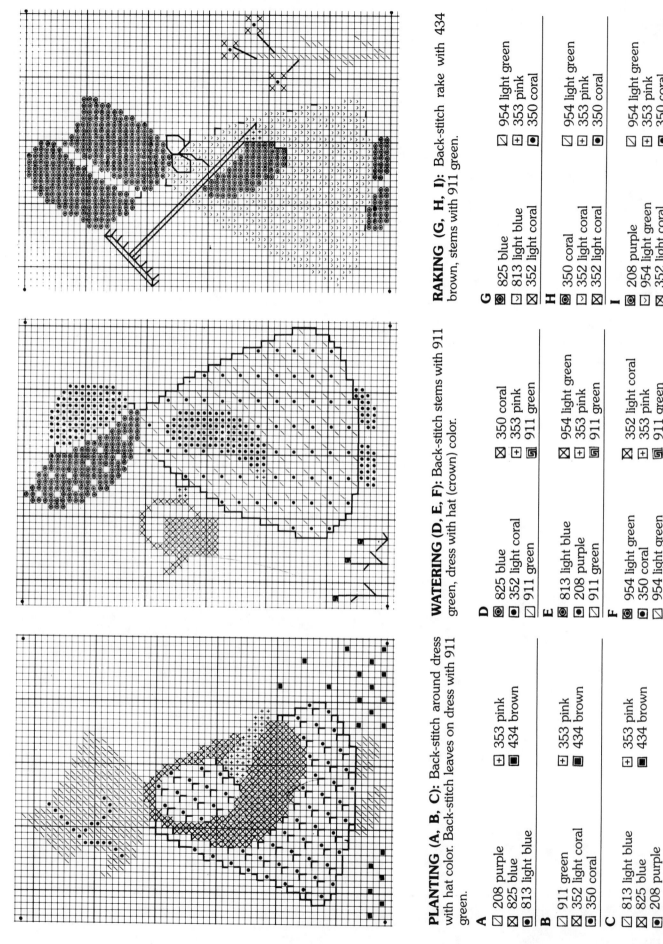

PLANTING (A, B, C): Back-stitch around dress with hat color. Back-stitch leaves on dress with 911 green.

A
☐ 208 purple	⊞ 353 pink
☒ 825 blue	■ 434 brown
⦿ 813 light blue	

B
☐ 911 green	⊞ 353 pink
☒ 352 light coral	■ 434 brown
⦿ 350 coral	

C
☐ 813 light blue	⊞ 353 pink
☒ 825 blue	■ 434 brown
⦿ 208 purple	

WATERING (D, E, F): Back-stitch stems with 911 green, dress with hat (crown) color.

D
⊚ 825 blue	☒ 350 coral
⦿ 352 light coral	⊞ 353 pink
☐ 911 green	⑤ 911 green

E
⊚ 813 light blue	☒ 954 light green
⦿ 208 purple	⊞ 353 pink
☐ 911 green	⑤ 911 green

F
⊚ 954 light green	☒ 352 light coral
⦿ 350 coral	⊞ 353 pink
☐ 954 light green	⑤ 911 green

RAKING (G, H, I): Back-stitch rake with 434 brown, stems with 911 green.

G
⦿ 825 blue	☐ 954 light green
☐ 813 light blue	⊞ 353 pink
☒ 352 light coral	⦿ 350 coral

H
⦿ 350 coral	☐ 954 light green
☐ 352 light coral	⊞ 353 pink
☒ 352 light coral	⦿ 350 coral

I
⦿ 208 purple	☐ 954 light green
☐ 954 light green	⊞ 353 pink
☒ 352 light coral	⦿ 350 coral

PLANTING

WATERING

RAKING

BLOOMING

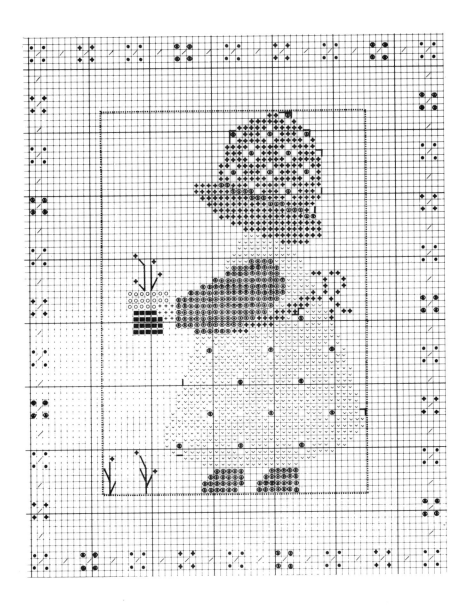

BLOOMING (J, K, L): Work all flowers with 208 purple, back-stitch stems with 911 green

J

⊞	954 light green	⊡	729 gold
◑	350 coral	⊕	353 pink
☑	352 light coral	◼	434 brown

K

⊞	208 purple	⊡	729 gold
◑	825 blue	⊕	353 pink
☑	813 light blue	◼	434 brown

L

⊞	352 light coral	⊡	729 gold
◑	813 light blue	⊕	353 pink
☑	954 light green	◼	434 brown

BORDER (FOR ALL VARIATIONS):

◉	350 coral
⊞	208 purple
◎	825 blue
⊘	954 light green

11

Stenciling

Stenciling is one of those wonderful early American crafts that blends so well with the craft of quilt making. If you think that the stenciled quilt is a new idea dreamed up this year by an overly ambitious crafts person, you're wrong! The stenciled bedcovering is over 150 years old and was very popular during that period in our history when stencilers put their designs on floors, walls and furniture.

STENCILING HOW-TO

THE STENCILS

Special plastic stencil paper which is available at most craft stores can be used to make your stencils. You can also use a medium weight tag paper (such as is used to make office file folders) for your stencils if you treat this paper. First transfer the stencil design to the paper (use carbon paper for this). Mix equal parts of boiled linseed oil and turpentine. You'll need about ½ cup. Dip a paper towel in the linseed oil/turpentine mixture and apply it to both sides of your stencil page. Be sure that the stencil is completely saturated. Hang the treated stencil to dry; it will probably take about ½ hour. Work in a well-ventilated room and use a clean paper towel for each stencil. Immediately after the stencil has been treated, drop the paper towel in water and then destroy it. Don't save the paper towels for later use. Remember that turpentine is highly flammable. Do not use near open flame, such as lighted cigarette.

STENCIL-CUTTING KNIVES

A stencil knife is usually used to cut stencils. You can, however, get excellent results with a craft knife (we use an X-Acto No. 1) and a sharp blade. (If possible, replace your regular blade with a No. 10 curved blade.) Keep a supply of blades on hand and be prepared to change blades if your cutting starts to get jagged.

STENCIL BRUSHES

Paint is applied to the stencil with a round brush (*Fig 1*). You can buy regular stencil brushes, or you can use any cylindrical brush such as a gluing brush. If you are planning to do a great deal of stenciling, you will want to buy brushes of different diameters to use for large and small areas. (For our quilt, three medium-sized brushes will be sufficient.) Wrap some masking tape around the brush so that only about ½" at the very end is exposed as in *Fig 2*. (This will help to keep the brush firm.) Your brush must be clean and completely dry for each color. If you want to use just one brush, remember it may take 24 hours for it to dry completely between colors.

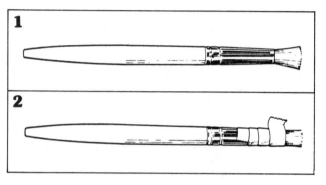

STENCIL PAINT

Many different kinds of paint can be used for stenciling in general and stenciling on fabric in particular. Despite what the ads say, you do not need any special stencil paint, although if this type of paint is available to you, you can use it. The best thing to use for stenciling on fabric is fabric paint. This kind of paint is sold under many different brand names and is available at craft shops or departments, art supply stores, or even paint shops. After the paint has dried, many of these fabric paints must be set with a hot iron to make the color permanent. Follow the manufacturer's directions. Regular artists' acrylic paints in tubes or jars can also be used for fabric stenciling. These paints are permanent and washable.

CUTTING THE STENCIL

Three different colors are used to make our stenciled blocks (see key on page 16) so you will need to cut three stencils for each block, one for each color.

If you are cutting plastic stencils, lay the plastic over the stencil designs on pages 16 to 19. Trace the *entire* design onto a separate plastic sheet for each color. Use a permanent marker for your tracing lines. If you wish, you may use a different color marker for each color.

If you are cutting cardboard stencils, lay a sheet of tracing paper over the design in the book and trace the design. Then use this tracing to transfer design with carbon paper onto cardboard. While it is possible to trace directly from this book, we do not recommend it because the page could tear thereby rendering the design on the reverse unusable. Treat cardboard as described above.

Step 1: A firm surface for cutting the stencil is a must. The best surface is a piece of glass (be sure the edges are taped), but you can use a pile of newspapers, a piece of wood, vinyl floor tile, a stack of magazines; anything you don't mind marring and knicking with knife cuts.

Step 2: Place your stencil on the cutting surface and grasp your knife as if you were holding a pencil, but be prepared to apply a little more pressure than when just drawing a straight line. You will cut out the shaded areas for one color leaving the other areas intact. Cut only the green areas on one stencil; only the red areas on the second stencil and only the yellow areas on the third stencil. The complete design on each stencil is used to register your other colors. Cut small areas first; large areas last. This will keep the stencil intact and prevent weakening the narrow joining areas.

Step 3: Place your new, sharp blade on one of the cutting lines and start to cut. Now for the trick to cutting successful stencils. **Try to keep the hand holding the cutting knife as motionless as possible.** Use your other hand to move the paper continuously. You should be cutting toward your body so keep turning the stencil with your other hand so that you can cut towards your body at all times. Cut in long motions, trying never to lift the blade. Lifting the blade can produce jagged edges. If you have difficulty moving the paper, you may need a harder cutting surface.

Step 4: Try always to cut from the outside of a pattern toward the center. Since the center is removed, it won't matter if you make extra cuts as in *Fig 3*. If you go off a line, don't lift your knife and stop. Merely cut back to the line. If the knife slips and you make too large a cut, use a little masking tape to mend the tear.

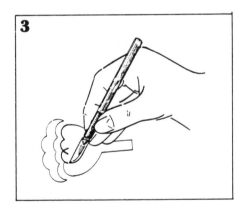

PAINTING THE STENCIL

Step 1: A fabric of 100% cotton works best for stenciling. Make sure that the grain of all fabric is straight. Wash the fabric to remove any sizing, and iron to get rid of wrinkles. Pull your fabric as tight as possible and tape in position so that it will not move. You may want to cover your working area with newspaper or paper towels and then place a blotter under your fabric. The blotter absorbs excess paint and helps to hold the fabric to the surface.

Step 2: Center the stencil on the fabric and tape securely. If the stencil is not secure, the pounding of the stencil brush can cause the stencil to shift, and the resulting design will be smeared.

Step 3: Now comes the fun part: applying the paint! The secret here is to use as little paint as possible. There is no such thing in stenciling as "too little paint." Dip the bottom edge of the bristles into the paint. Now have a supply of newspapers or paper towels at your side and then pound the brush on the newspaper or paper towels in an up-and-down motion to get rid of excess paint. This is called "pouncing." When very little paint is left on the brush, you are ready to apply the brush to the stencil. **Successful stenciling is done with practically no paint on the brush.**

Step 4: Hold the stencil down with your hand so that it doesn't slip, and hold the stencil brush in the other hand as you would a pencil, but work with the brush perpendicular to the fabric as in *Fig 4.* Apply the paint with a rapid up-and-down motion. You don't want to simply cover the fabric with paint; you want to pound the paint into the fabric. Work from the outside edge of a shape toward the center. This will keep the paint from seeping under the stencil. Keep working with very little paint on the brush. When the brush is completely dry, repeat the process of pouncing. Don't lift up the stencil until you are completely through applying a color.

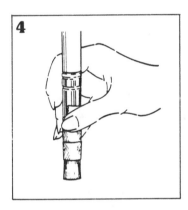

Step 5: You shouldn't be controlling the amount of paint by pounding heavily at some areas and lighter at others. The pounding should be a heavy stroke at all times. The control comes from working with a little bit of paint at all times! If you have applied too much paint, you will find that you have trouble lifting the stencil when you are finished, and paint will run under the stencil.

Step 6: Make sure that one color has dried before applying the second color. Use a clean, dry brush for each color. After you have applied all of your colors, let the fabric dry for about twenty-four hours before you proceed to make the rest of the quilt. Occasionally you will want to clean your stencil—especially if you have an accumulation of paint. Wipe the stencil with a paper towel dipped in water or turpentine (depending on whether you are using a water-based or turpentine-based paint). Always make sure that no paint has gathered on the underside of the stencil. In addition, keep your fingers free of paint so that you have no smudges on your quilt block. If a bit of paint gets on the block, remove it at once before it has a chance to dry.

EARLY AMERICAN STENCIL QUILT

Four authentic old-time applique quilt designs make up this magnificent quilt. If you'd like to practice stenciling but don't want to tackle as big a project as a quilt, you can use the individual stencils to make pillows and other small projects as shown in the photo.

Size

Approx 81″ × 96″

Materials for Quilt

All fabric requirements are based on 44″–45″ wide material. If you are using narrower fabric, adjust yardage accordingly. (Try to get 100% cotton or a blend with no more than 30% synthetic.)
5 yds natural fabric (*for blocks, border and binding*)
1⅓ yds green fabric (*for framing*)
3 yds red print fabric (*for sashing and borders*)
85″ × 100″ sheet polyester quilt batting
5¾ yds backing fabric
Fabric shears
Sewing and quilting needles
Sewing and quilting thread
Beeswax
Straight pins
Iron
Quilting hoop or frame
Thimble
Water-soluble marking pen

Before beginning to work, wash and iron all fabrics to be used in the quilt. Make sure that the grain of all fabric is straight and that the fabric is colorfast.

Materials for Stenciling

Plastic for stencils
    or
Medium-weight cardboard and turpentine, boiled
    linseed oil, and paper towels
Stencil or craft knife
Blades
Firm cutting surface
Red, yellow and green paints
3 Stencil brushes (*one for each color*)
Blotter
Newspapers
Bowls

Instructions

Step 1: Cut a piece of natural fabric 14″ × 14″ for each block. Iron the block so that it is smooth. Find the center of your fabric by folding it in half vertically and horizontally. Mark center to aid you in placing the stencil. Use a pin or small piece of masking tape. Do not use a marker which may be covered with paint.

Step 2: Prepare the work surface by covering an area with newspapers or paper towels and a blotter. This will absorb the excess paint, and in addition, the blotter will help to hold the fabric to the surface. Tape the block to the work

surface, pulling it as tight as possible. Make certain that the fabric is secure and can't move.

Step 3: Following the directions on page 13, for stenciling make five blocks of each stencil. The charts on pages 16 to 19 show what colors we used on our quilt blocks. Feel free to substitute colors of your own choosing. Follow the manufacturer's directions for setting the color.

Step 4: Prepare the second border, which is the stenciled border. From the prewashed natural fabric, cut four strips, each 10″ wide. Cut two 90½″ long (for the sides of the quilt) and two 87½″ long (for the top and bottom of the quilt). Although the border strips will actually be 6½″ wide by 78½″ long (for the sides) and 6½″ × 75½″ (for the top and bottom), this extra material will make it easier to stencil. Fold the strips in half lengthwise and crosswise to locate the centers in both directions. Mark this line at several points in both directions. Be sure to use a marking instrument which can be removed easily, such as a water-soluble erasable marking pen, chalk, etc. You will need this line to place your stencil. Starting in the center, mark off 6″ long blocks as in *Fig 1*. The repeats will be placed in these blocks. You will have 13 repeats on the side borders and eleven repeats on the top and bottom borders. Iron the strips so that they are smooth.

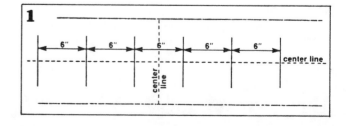

Step 5: Prepare the work surface as you did for the blocks and tape the strip to the surface. The border is stenciled with the flower and leaf motif from the "President's Wreath" block. Alternate the left flower with the right flower. Center the motif in the 6″ block, placing the flower so that the bottom edge of the stem is on the center line as in *Fig 2*.

Stencil the borders as you did the blocks. Follow the manufacturer's directions for setting the color.

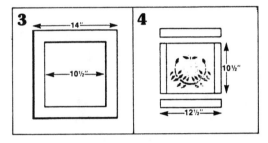

Step 6: Following the instructions for blocking on page 5, block each quilt square to a perfect 10½″ square. Cut your cardboard template with a 10½″ square opening as in *Fig 3*.

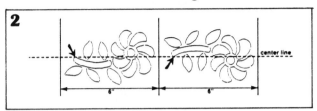

Step 7: From the green framing fabric, cut 40 strips, each 1½″ wide and 10½″ long and 40 strips 1½″ wide and 12½″ long. Frame the blocks as described on page 5 (*Fig 4*).

Step 8: From the red sashing fabric, cut sixteen sashing strips, 3½″ wide by 12½″ long. Look at *Fig 5* for the arrangement of blocks. *NOTE: Be sure the top of each design is in the right position.*

Place sashing strip (*Fig 5: No. 1*) across the bottom of a "President's Wreath" block right sides together and stitch with the ¼″ seam allowance. Then sew same piece of sashing to top of a "Prairie Flower" block. In same manner stitch second sashing strip (*Fig 5: No. 2*) to bottom of "Prairie Flower" block and then to top of a "President's Wreath" block. Join sashing strip (*Fig 5: No. 3*) to bottom of "President's Wreath" block and to top of a "Prairie Flower" block.

Join sashing strip (*Fig 5: No. 4*) to bottom of "Prairie Flower" block and to top of a "President's Wreath" block.

You now have a vertical strip of five joined blocks. Following *Fig 5* for placement, make three more vertical strips in same manner. You now have four vertical strips each measuring about 72½″ (which includes ¼″ seam allowance at top and bottom). Press all seams to one side before joining next seam.

Cut three sashing strips, each 3½″ wide and 72½″ long. Attach these three strips (*Fig 5: Nos. 17, 18 and 19*) on the side of each row of blocks. Now attach strips together

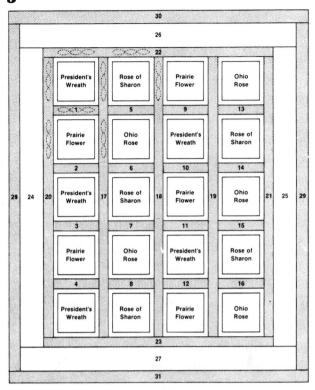

following the order in *Fig 5*. Do this very carefully so that all blocks line up. Again, carefully press all seams to one side before joining the next seam.

Step 9: Now add the first border, made from the red print fabric. Cut four border strips, each 3½″ wide. Cut two 72½″ long (or length of your quilt top) and two 63½″ long (or width of your quilt top). In same manner as for vertical sashing, sew two longer border strips to right and left sides of quilt top (*Fig 5: Nos. 20 and 21*). Then sew shorter border strips to top and bottom (*Fig 5: Nos. 22 and 23*). Press all seams to one side.

Step 10: Border Two is the stenciled border which is prepared in step 4. Cut your stenciled border to the correct length and width measuring from the centers out. All four strips should be 6½″ wide. Two are 78½″ long (or length of quilt top) and two 75½″ (or width of quilt top). Attach two longer border strips to right and left sides of quilt top (*Fig 5: Nos. 24 and 25*) and shorter strips to top and bottom (*Fig 5: Nos. 26 and 27*). Press all seams to one side.

Step 11: Border Three is again made of the red print fabric. From this fabric cut four border strips, each 3½″ wide. Cut two 90½″ long (or length of quilt top) and two 81½″ (or width of quilt top). Attach two longer strips to right and left sides of quilt top (*Fig 5: Nos. 28 and 29*) and shorter strips to top and bottom (*Fig 5: Nos. 30 and 31*). Give top a final steaming, making sure all corners are square and that all seams are pressed to one side.

Step 12: Quilt or tie top and attach binding, following directions on page 6.

PRESIDENT'S WREATH

ROSE OF SHARON

17

PRAIRIE FLOWER

OHIO ROSE

Chicken Scratch™

It was during the dark days of the Great Depression. A poor farm wife wanted desperately to trim her gingham dress with a bit of lace. But lace was so expensive! All she had were a few skeins of embroidery floss and her imagination. She set to work.

From across the room, her husband questioned what she was doing.

"I'm putting lace on my dress," she answered as she began embroidering a few dark Double Cross stitches on her gingham.

"Looks like a lot of chicken scratches to me," he replied.

* * *

We're not sure if the story is true, but we'd like to believe it because it makes such a romantic beginning to the lovely craft that is today called Chicken Scratch™, or Snowflaking, or Depression Lace, or Hoover Lace, or—sometimes—Gingham Lace.

Chicken Scratch™ is a trademark of Pegasus Originals, Inc.

CHICKEN SCRATCH™ HOW TO

THE FABRIC

Chicken Scratch™ is worked on gingham fabric, either the regular gingham yardage found in fabric departments, or special evenweave gingham embroidery fabrics (such as Gerda or Guilford Gingham) found at needlework specialty shops or departments. Either works well. The quilt shown here has been worked on gingham; the other projects are worked on evenweave.

The squares of evenweave gingham are perfectly square. But beware; the squares of regular gingham yardage are not. When the selvage is at the side of the fabric, the blocks will be slightly taller than wide. Our charts are made to allow for this difference.

Gingham yardage usually comes in 4, 8 or 16 squares to the inch. (For Chicken Scratch™, eight stitches to the inch is the most popular size, and our quilt has been worked in this fabric.) Remember, however, that this measurement will be accurate in only one direction. A fabric will be 8 squares to the inch in one direction but approximately 7 in the other.

The number of squares in each inch of fabric will determine the finished size of your work. Our designs are 57, 58 or 59 squares long and wide. When worked on eight to the inch gingham, the Chicken Scratch™ area will be approx-

imately 7⅜″ × 8½″. When working projects from other charts, always count the number of squares you need, instead of measuring by inches.

To determine the size of evenweave fabric required, divide the number of squares per inch of fabric into the number of squares of the design. For example, if your fabric has eight squares to the inch, to work a design 64 × 64 squares, you will need a working area of about 8″ square. For regular gingham, figure the length and width separately. For example, to work the same design on eight to the inch gingham, you will need a working area of about 8″ × 9″.

If you are working a large project—such as our quilt—make sure that the selvage is always in the same place (either at the sides or the top) to ensure that the taller squares will always be running in the same direction. Our quilt was worked with the selvages at the sides. Before starting to stitch, always wash and iron the fabric to remove any sizing and allow for shrinkage.

THE THREAD

Six-strand cotton embroidery floss is generally used. You can, however, experiment with other threads. Pearl cotton used for all or part of the design is elegant, and crochet cotton used in place of white floss adds dimension.

Generally two strands of floss are used in the needle with regular gingham yardage. Evenweave gingham is usually worked with three.

Anchor the thread by weaving it through stitches on the back, and start a new thread by working over it on the back for the first few stitches. Although in most embroidery, knots are to be avoided, if you are doing a Chicken Scratch™ project that will receive a lot of wear, or that will be washed frequently, we suggest you use a small knot to begin and end each thread.

NEEDLES

A size 24 tapestry needle (blunt pointed) can be used on both the evenweave and regular gingham yardage. The blunt-pointed size 24 is small enough to pierce the regular gingham easily and keeps you from sticking your fingers when working the Woven Wheel. If you prefer a sharp point, use a size 7 or 8 crewel needle.

HOOPS

Chicken Scratch™ must be worked with the fabric stretched fairly tightly in a hoop. The hoop should have a screw closure to ensure the proper tension (spring hoops will not hold the fabric tight enough). Place the fabric in the hoop so that it is held tightly, but so that the squares are not stretched or distorted (a gentle tug here and there will help keep it square).

THE STITCHES

Only three stitches are used for Chicken Scratch™: Double Cross, Straight, and Woven Wheel. *In all of the following diagrams, bring needle up at 1 and all odd numbers, down at 2 and all even numbers.*

As you work, keep your tension firm, but not so tight that the fabric is distorted or puckered.

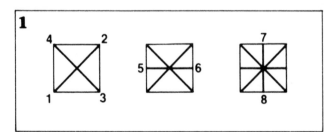

DOUBLE CROSS STITCH: This is used both to outline and to fill in design areas. It is usually worked with dark thread on white squares, and with white thread on dark squares (***Fig 1***). Take care to work Step 1 in the exact corners of the square, and Steps 2 and 3 in the exact vertical and horizontal centers. Complete all three steps of each Double Cross Stitch before moving on to the next. Double Cross Stitch worked with dark thread on the white squares will outline the design as in the First Step of ***Plate 1.*** Double Cross Stitch worked with white thread on the dark squares will fill in the design area as shown in the Second Step of ***Plate 1. HINT: When two stitches meet, be sure to make them "hold hands" or share the same hole (**Fig 2**).*

Plate 1
REGULAR CHICKEN SCRATCH™

Step 1: Work dark Double Cross Stitches.

Step 2: Work light Double Cross Stitches.

Step 3: Work Straight Stitches.

Step 4: Work Woven Wheels.

Plate 2
REVERSE CHICKEN SCRATCH™

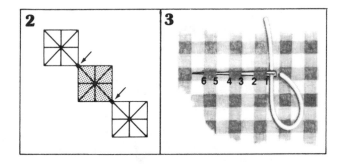

STRAIGHT STITCH: This stitch, usually worked with white on the medium squares, forms the "arms" around which the wheel is woven. Four arms, two vertical and two horizontal, are required for each wheel. Straight stitch works up quickly when done as for basting: running the needle over a medium square, then under a white square, then over and under again (**Fig 3**).

Work the straight stitches with a medium tension, not too tightly. This will make the weaving easier. Your work now looks like the Third Step in **Plate 1**.

HINT: For ease in working the vertical straight stitch, turn your work sideways and work vertical running rows in same manner as horizontal running rows.

When working on a large project, you may work all of the required Straight stitches and then begin on the Woven Wheels; or you may prefer to work the Straight stitches in a specific area, then complete the Woven Wheel stitches in that same area. This latter method of working leaves less chance for error in placement of straight stitches.

WOVEN WHEEL: Now for the fun! This is the magic stitch that will turn your work into lovely lace!

The stitch is worked entirely on the surface of the fabric, with the needle going under the four arms previously formed by the straight stitches.

Thread your needle with double the number of strands (four strands for regular gingham; six strands for evenweave).

Step 1: Bring needle up at 1, in the exact hole as the first arm is worked.

Step 2: Working counter-clockwise, bring needle around and under all four arms, adjusting tension to form a circle or wheel. If you are left-handed, you will probably find it easier to work in a clockwise direction.

Step 3: Bring needle down through fabric at 1 (**Fig 4**). Your work now looks like the Fourth Step in **Plate 1**.

HINT: If you prefer not changing the number of strands in your needle, weave thread around the circle twice.

WORKING REVERSE CHICKEN SCRATCH™

Reverse Chicken Scratch™ uses the same stitches and all of the same techniques. The only difference is the use of dark thread to form the "lace." The Double Cross stitches are worked with white floss on the dark squares to form the outline of the design. Then the design area is filled in with dark thread, and the Straight stitches and the Woven Wheel are both worked with dark thread. Reverse Chicken Scratch™ is shown in **Plate 2**.

STITCHING FROM CHARTS

Our designs are charted on gingham background, to make them easier to follow. Note that gingham has three color gradations: dark (the solid color used in the weaving, such as blue); light (always white); and medium, which is a blend of the color with the white.

Each square on the chart equals one square of gingham. Symbols are placed on the squares to show what stitch and color to use. The symbols we use are:

- ♣ Dark Double Cross
- ✿ Light Double Cross
- ▬ Dark Straight Stitch (horizontal)
- – Light Straight Stitch (horizontal)
- ▮ Dark Straight Stitch (vertical)
- ⎮ Light Straight Stitch (vertical)
- ◉ Dark Woven Wheel
- ○ Light Woven Wheel

Arrows are placed at the top and side of each chart to help you find the center, and we also give you the maximum size, in squares of each design.

LET'S PRACTICE

Before starting to work on your quilt, you may want to work these practice charts—one for regular Chicken Scratch™ and the other for reverse—to be sure you understand the stitches and to get the feel of the correct tension for your stitches. This practice piece will also show you the order in which to work the stitches.

*HINT: Before stitching, make it a practice to mark the top of your work with a small safety pin or a stitch with a contrasting color. As you work you will be turning the fabric, and this will let you easily find the top again. **Plate 1** shows you what each step should look like when completed. **Plate 2** shows you completed Reverse Chicken Scratch™.*

PRACTICE CHARTS:

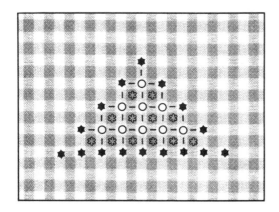

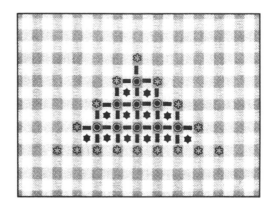

REGULAR CHICKEN SCRATCH℠

Step 1: Work all of the dark Double Cross Stitches (✦).
Step 2: Work all of the light Double Cross Stitches (✿).
Step 3: Work the Straight Stitches (— and │).
Step 4: Work the Woven Wheels (◯).

REVERSE CHICKEN SCRATCH℠

Step 1: Work all of the light Double Cross Stitches (✦).
Step 2: Work all of the dark Double Cross Stitches (✿).
Step 3: Work the Straight Stitches (▬ and ▮).
Step 4: Work the Woven Wheels (◉).

CHICKEN SCRATCH℠ QUILT

Actual quilt block designs have been translated into charts for working this delightful Chicken Scratch℠ quilt. If you prefer, you can, of course, use these designs to make other projects such as the pillows we show here.

Size

Approx 51″ × 67″

Materials and Equipment

All fabric requirements are based on 44″–45″ wide material. If you are using narrower fabric, adjust yardage accordingly.

5 yds gingham fabric (*for blocks, sashing, borders and binding*)
16 yds 2″ white insertion lace (*for framing*)
1 yd white fabric (*for framing*)
4 yds fabric (*for backing*)
   (*NOTE: Gingham can be used for backing*)
1 package twin size quilt batting
24 skeins white embroidery floss
24 skeins blue embroidery floss
Fabric shears and embroidery scissors
Sewing, Chicken Scratching℠ and quilting needles
Sewing and quilting thread (*white is preferred*)
Beeswax
Embroidery hoop
Quilting hoop or frame
Straight pins
Iron
Thimble
Water-soluble marking pen

Before cutting, wash and iron all fabrics. Make sure that grain of fabric is straight.

NOTE: The quilt pictured here makes up a small comforter, crib quilt or wall hanging. If you prefer a larger covering suitable for a twin or double bed, make twenty Chicken Scratch™ blocks by repeating eight of your favorite designs. Then set the blocks four across and five down. This will make a quilt measuring 67" × 83". Fabric, trimming and floss requirements for this quilt are:

8 yds gingham fabric (*for blocks, sashing, borders, binding*)
27 yds white insertion lace (*for framing*)
1⅓ yds white fabric (*for framing*)
5 yds backing fabric
40 skeins white embroidery floss
40 skeins blue embroidery floss

Instructions

Step 1: Cut a 14" square from the gingham fabric for each block. Fold block fabric in half and then in half again to find approximate center. Follow arrows on chart to find center of chart and mark this on fabric. Use this center square as starting point for counting.

Step 2: Work Chicken Scratching™, following instructions on pages 21-22. When Chicken Scratching™ has been completed, wash block, place face down on a terry towel on ironing board and steam dry. This will make embroidery "stand up." Do not let iron rest on stitches; let steam do the work!

Step 3: Following instructions for blocking on page 5, block each quilt block to a perfect 10½" square. Cut your cardboard template with a 10½" square opening as in **Fig 1**.

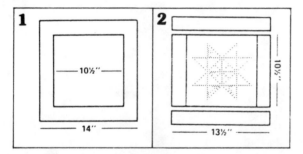

Step 4: The framing for the block is made of insertion lace mounted on a strip of gingham. From the framing fabric cut 24 strips, each 2" wide and 10½" long and 24 strips, 2" wide × 13½" long. Now cut 24 strips of insertion lace, each 10½" long, and 24 strips, 13½" long. Right sides up, lay the insertion lace over the framing fabric and pin. Work with lace and framing as one. Frame the blocks as described on page 5 (**Fig 2**).

Step 5: From sashing fabric, cut nine sashing strips, 3½" wide × 13½" long. *NOTE: Be sure that the top of each design is in the right position.* Place sashing strip (**Fig 3: No. 1**) across bottom of "Basket" block right sides together and stitch. Then sew same piece of sashing to top of

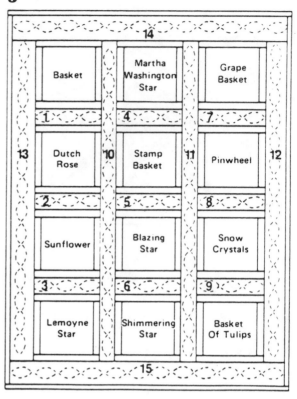

"Dutch Rose" block. In same manner stitch second sashing strip (**Fig 3: No. 2**) to bottom of "Dutch Rose" block and then to top of "Sunflower" block. Join third sashing strip (**Fig 3: No. 3**) to bottom of "Sunflower" block and to top of "Lemoyne Star" block. You now have a vertical strip of four joined blocks. Following **Fig 3** for placement, make two more vertical strips in same manner. You now have three vertical strips each measuring about 61½" (which includes ¼" seam allowance at top and bottom). Press all seams to one side before joining next seam. Cut two sashing strips, each 3½" wide and 61" long (or length of your strip of blocks). Sew one strip to each side of center row of blocks (**Fig 3: Nos. 10 and 11**). Sew first and third row of blocks to these same strips, being sure that tops and bottoms of all blocks line up exactly. Press seams.

Step 6: Now complete quilt top by adding borders to top, bottom and sides. Cut four border strips, each 3½" wide. Cut two 61½" long (or length of your quilt top) and two 51½" wide (or width of your quilt top). In same manner as for vertical sashing, sew two longer border strips to right and left sides of quilt top (**Fig 3: Nos. 12 and 13**). Then sew shorter border strips to top and bottom (**Fig 3: Nos. 14 and 15**). Give quilt top final steaming, making sure all corners are square and that all seams are pressed to one side. Quilt top is now ready for quilting or tying.

Step 7: Quilt or tie top and attach binding following directions on page 6.

BASKET
58 squares × 58 squares

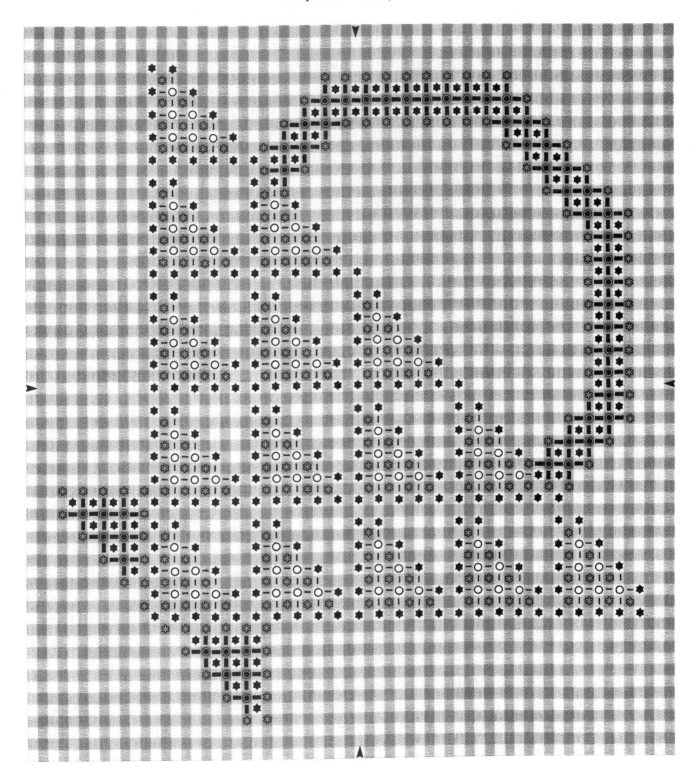

COLOR KEY

♣ = Dark Double Cross

✿ = Light Double Cross

■ = Dark Straight Stitch *(horizontal)*

– = Light Straight Stitch *(horizontal)*

❚ = Dark Straight Stitch *(vertical)*

ı = Light Straight Stitch *(vertical)*

◉ = Dark Woven Wheel

○ = Light Woven Wheel

MARTHA WASHINGTON STAR
57 squares × 57 squares

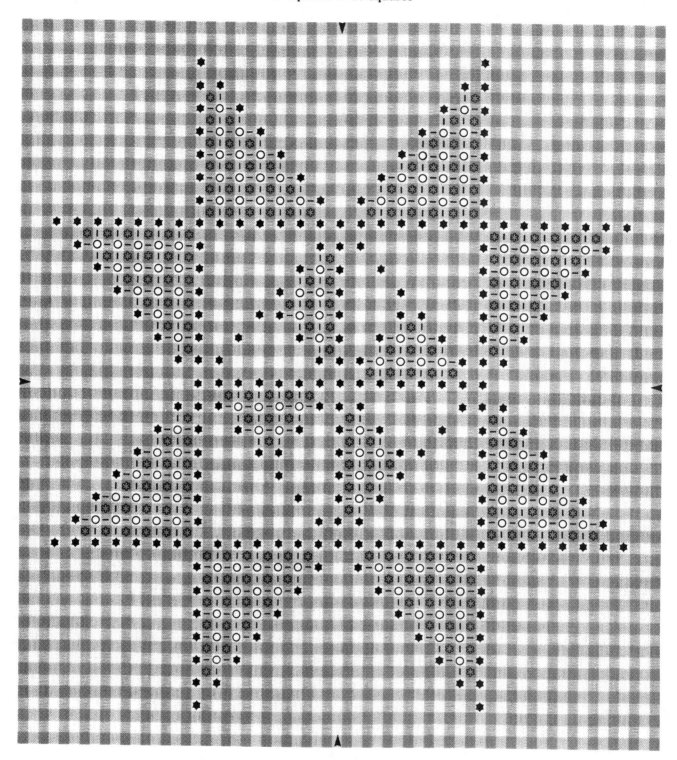

COLOR KEY

- ✦ = Dark Double Cross
- ✿ = Light Double Cross
- ▬ = Dark Straight Stitch *(horizontal)*
- – = Light Straight Stitch *(horizontal)*
- ▮ = Dark Straight Stitch *(vertical)*
- | = Light Straight Stitch *(vertical)*
- ◉ = Dark Woven Wheel
- ○ = Light Woven Wheel

GRAPE BASKET
58 squares × 58 squares

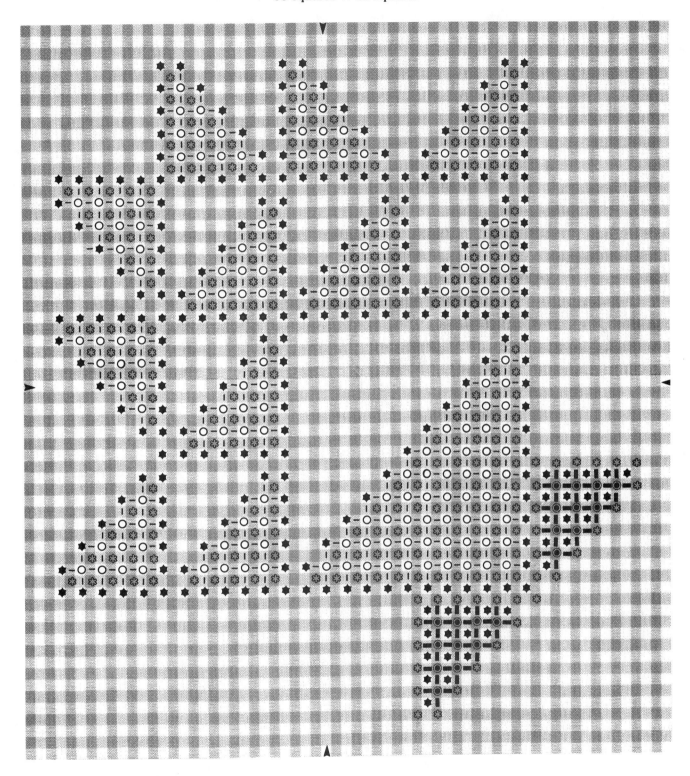

COLOR KEY

✿ = Dark Double Cross

❀ = Light Double Cross

■■ = Dark Straight Stitch *(horizontal)*

– = Light Straight Stitch *(horizontal)*

❚ = Dark Straight Stitch *(vertical)*

❘ = Light Straight Stitch *(vertical)*

◉ = Dark Woven Wheel

○ = Light Woven Wheel

27

DUTCH ROSE
57 squares × 57 squares

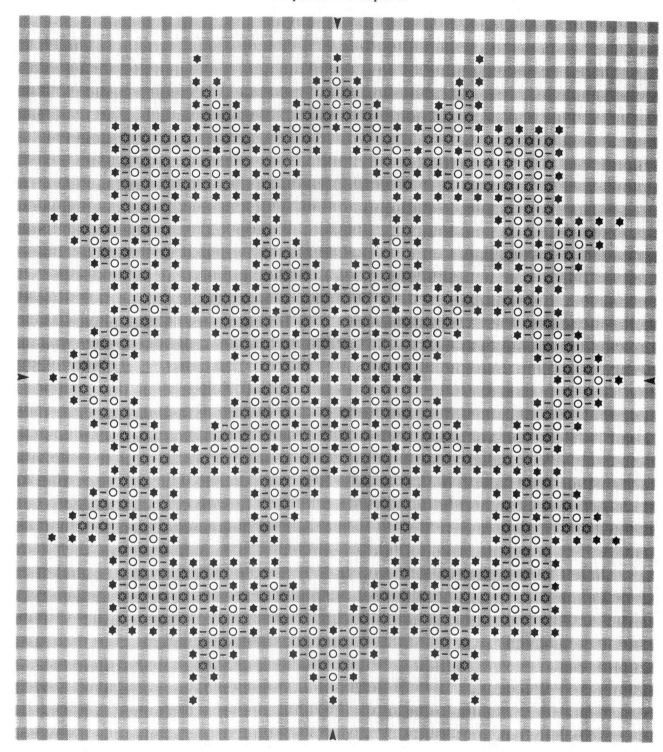

COLOR KEY

✿ = Dark Double Cross

✾ = Light Double Cross

▬ = Dark Straight Stitch *(horizontal)*

− = Light Straight Stitch *(horizontal)*

▌ = Dark Straight Stitch *(vertical)*

| = Light Straight Stitch *(vertical)*

◉ = Dark Woven Wheel

○ = Light Woven Wheel

STAMP BASKET

59 squares × 59 squares

COLOR KEY

♣ = Dark Double Cross

❀ = Light Double Cross

■— = Dark Straight Stitch *(horizontal)*

— = Light Straight Stitch *(horizontal)*

▮= Dark Straight Stitch *(vertical)*

|= Light Straight Stitch *(vertical)*

◉= Dark Woven Wheel

○= Light Woven Wheel

29

PINWHEEL
57 squares × 57 squares

COLOR KEY

⬟ = Dark Double Cross

❀ = Light Double Cross

▬ = Dark Straight Stitch *(horizontal)*

– = Light Straight Stitch *(horizontal)*

❚ = Dark Straight Stitch *(vertical)*

I = Light Straight Stitch *(vertical)*

◉ = Dark Woven Wheel

○ = Light Woven Wheel

SUNFLOWER
57 squares × 57 squares

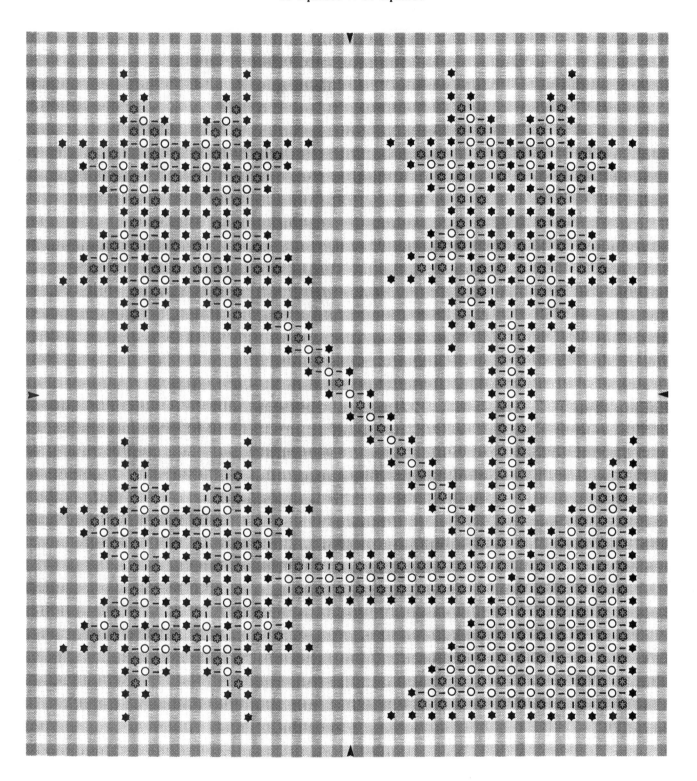

COLOR KEY

⬗ = Dark Double Cross

✿ = Light Double Cross

▬ = Dark Straight Stitch *(horizontal)*

− = Light Straight Stitch *(horizontal)*

▮ = Dark Straight Stitch *(vertical)*

| = Light Straight Stitch *(vertical)*

◉ = Dark Woven Wheel

○ = Light Woven Wheel

BLAZING STAR
57 squares × 57 squares

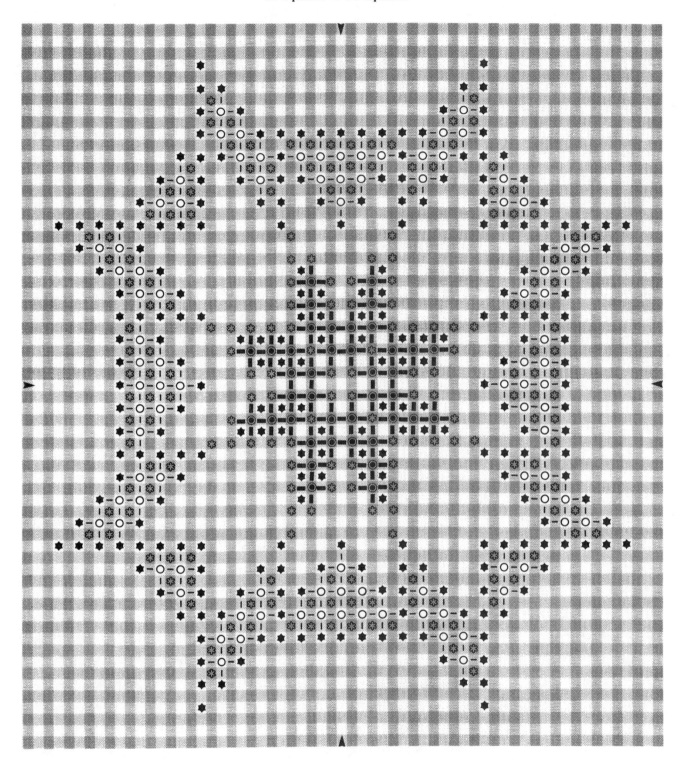

COLOR KEY

♣ = Dark Double Cross

❀ = Light Double Cross

▬ = Dark Straight Stitch *(horizontal)*

– = Light Straight Stitch *(horizontal)*

▮ = Dark Straight Stitch *(vertical)*

| = Light Straight Stitch *(vertical)*

◉ = Dark Woven Wheel

○ = Light Woven Wheel

SNOW CRYSTALS

57 squares × 57 squares

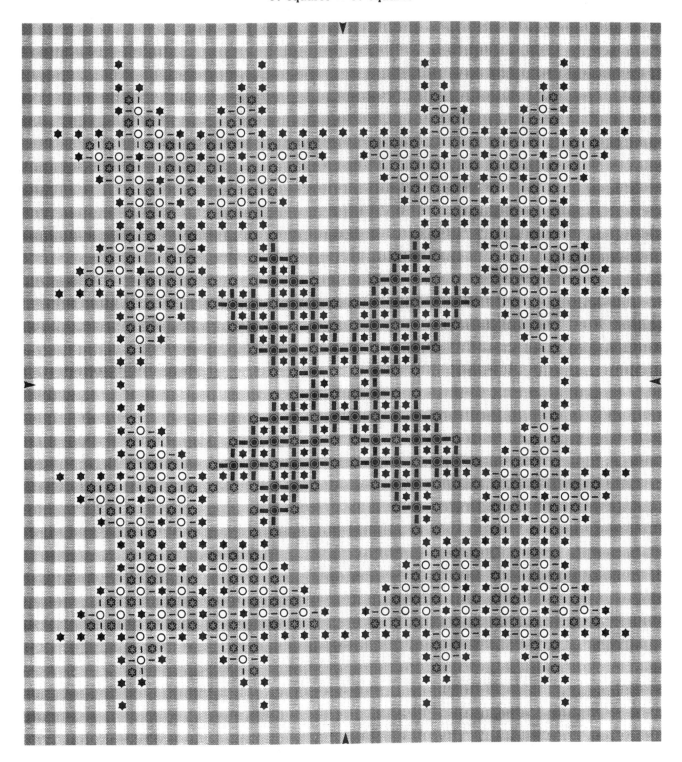

COLOR KEY

✿ = Dark Double Cross

❀ = Light Double Cross

■ = Dark Straight Stitch *(horizontal)*

– = Light Straight Stitch *(horizontal)*

▮ = Dark Straight Stitch *(vertical)*

| = Light Straight Stitch *(vertical)*

◉ = Dark Woven Wheel

○ = Light Woven Wheel

LEMOYNE STAR

57 squares × 57 squares

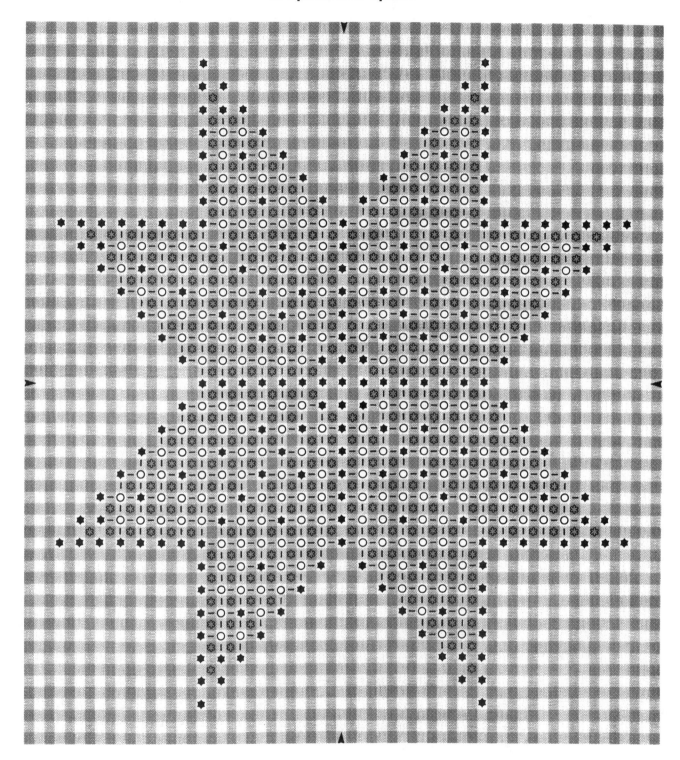

COLOR KEY

✦ = Dark Double Cross

✿ = Light Double Cross

▬ = Dark Straight Stitch *(horizontal)*

– = Light Straight Stitch *(horizontal)*

▐ = Dark Straight Stitch *(vertical)*

I = Light Straight Stitch *(vertical)*

◉ = Dark Woven Wheel

○ = Light Woven Wheel

SHIMMERING STAR

57 squares × 57 squares

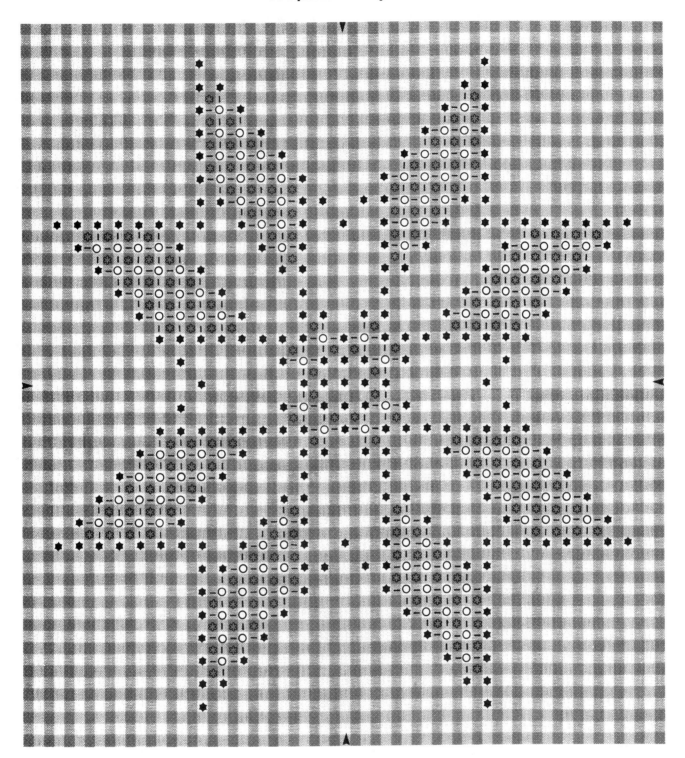

COLOR KEY

- ✦ = Dark Double Cross
- ✿ = Light Double Cross
- ▬ = Dark Straight Stitch *(horizontal)*
- ▬ = Light Straight Stitch *(horizontal)*
- ▐ = Dark Straight Stitch *(vertical)*
- | = Light Straight Stitch *(vertical)*
- ◉ = Dark Woven Wheel
- ○ = Light Woven Wheel

BASKET OF TULIPS

58 squares × 58 squares

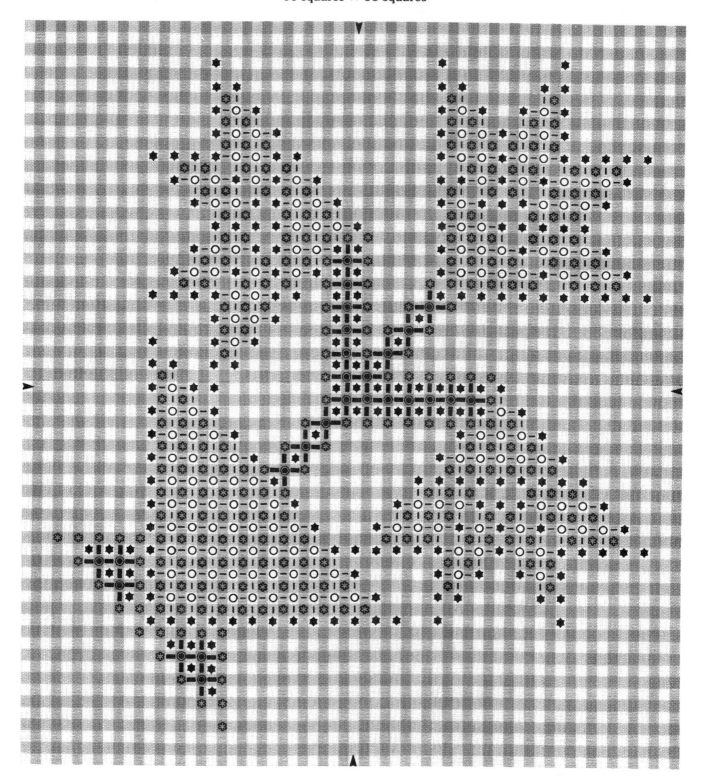

COLOR KEY

♣ = Dark Double Cross

✿ = Light Double Cross

▬ = Dark Straight Stitch *(horizontal)*

– = Light Straight Stitch *(horizontal)*

▮ = Dark Straight Stitch *(vertical)*

╷ = Light Straight Stitch *(vertical)*

◉ = Dark Woven Wheel

○ = Light Woven Wheel

Embroidery

If you like to embroider, what could be more fun than a quilt created with embroidered blocks!

You don't have to be an experienced embroiderer to create these heirloom quilts. We give you easy-to-follow stitch charts for each of the blocks. If you are an advanced embroiderer, you can use stitches of your own choice to make these quilts truly your own.

EMBROIDERY HOW-TO

THE FABRIC

Use a good quality 100% cotton in a pale color, such as a beige, for your quilt blocks. Before transferring your design, wash the fabric in hot water to remove sizing and to prevent any further shrinkage. If you have difficulty locating a 100% cotton in your color choice, you can use a blend, but try to find one that has no more than 30% synthetic fibers.

THE THREAD

Six-strand embroidery floss was used in all of our blocks. The strands can be separated and used in different combinations. Most of our stitches are worked with two strands of floss in the needle except French knots which are worked with four. You can, however, experiment with other threads. Pearl cotton used for all or part of the design is elegant.

Anchor the thread by weaving it through stitches on the back, and start a new thread by working over it on the back for the first few stitches. As in all fine embroidery, knots are to be avoided.

THE NEEDLES

You'll need a needle especially designed for embroidery such as a #6 or #8 Crewel needle.

THE HOOPS

Stretch the fabric in an embroidery hoop or frame. Keep the fabric taut for easy stitching.

THE STITCHES

While there are many embroidery stitches which could be used we have used only six easy stitches in our sample quilts. These are: French knot, Chain stitch, Satin stitch, Lazy Daisy (Detached Chain) stitch, Stem/outline stitch and Buttonhole Stitch.

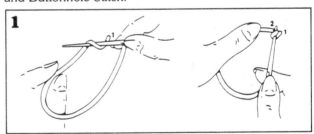

FRENCH KNOTS (worked with four strands): Bring needle up at 1, hold thread close to work with left thumb and index finger. Slip needle under thread, and turn needle clockwise. Still holding thread in left fingers, insert needle back down through fabric at 2, maintaining firm tension on thread until it is almost completely down through the fabric. (*Fig 1*).

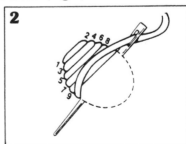

SATIN STITCH (worked with 2 strands): In the figure, needle comes up through work at 1, and all odd numbers, down at 2 and all even numbers. Keep tension even and the strands of thread smooth (*Fig 2*).

37

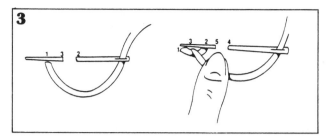

STEM/OUTLINE STITCH (worked with 2 strands):
In the figures, needle comes up through work at 1 and all odd numbers, down through fabric at 2 and all even numbers. Keep thread below needle at all times. At point 5, bring needle up and from now on always bring needle up through a previously used hole. Continue in this manner (**Fig 3**).

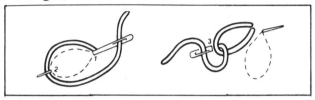

LAZY DAISY (DETACHED CHAIN) (worked with 2 strands): Bring needle up at 1, make a thread loop on surface to desired size, hold loop in place with left hand, while bringing needle down at 1 again (in same hole). Bring needle up at 2 and down at 3, tacking loop down with a short stitch (**Fig 4**).

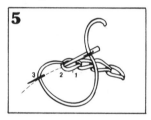

CHAIN STITCH (worked with 2 strands): Bring needle up at 1; make thread loop on top surface to desired size, hold loop in place with left hand, while bringing needle down again at 1 in same hole. Bring needle up at 2 and out at 3, bringing needle over yarn loop. Pull thread flat. Repeat across. Stitch can be worked from right to left or top to bottom (**Fig 5**).

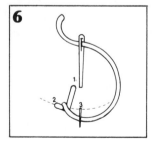

BUTTONHOLE STITCH (worked with 2 strands): Keeping thread below needle, come up at 1, down at 2, and up again at 3. Stitches can be placed close together or farther apart (**Fig 6**).

TRANSFERRING THE DESIGNS

The designs for each of the embroidered quilt blocks appear on pages 42 to 64 and 81. While it is possible to trace directly from this book, we do not recommend it because the page could tear thereby rendering the design on the reverse unusable.

Step 1: Prewash the fabric for the block. Iron the block flat so that it is smooth.

Step 2: Open book to desired pattern and lay book flat. A piece of white paper or cardboard placed under the page will be a help in seeing the pattern clearly. Lay a sheet of tracing paper over the design and carefully trace the pattern.

Step 3: Carefully position the tracing on the fabric and pin it at four corners.

Step 4: Place a large piece of cardboard on a flat surface, and place your fabric/tracing on it. The cardboard not only protects the surface but it also provides a firm padding under the fabric which will help in producing a nice, smooth line.

Step 5: Slip a sheet of dressmaker's carbon, color-side down between the tracing and the fabric. Do not pin the carbon in place.

(*NOTE: Do not use pencil or typewriter carbon as it will smudge and leave marks on the fabric which will be impossible to remove. Dressmaker's carbon, available at craft and fabric stores or departments, has a hard wax finish and is designed for transferring onto cloth.*)

Step 6: Using a hard, even pressure, trace a few lines with a dull pencil or a tracing wheel. Carefully remove one pin and gently lift one side of the tracing and check the impression. If the lines are too light, apply more pressure; too heavy less pressure. If the line is too heavy, it may be difficult to hide with embroidery and if the line is too light, it will be hard to see. The transfer does have a tendency to fade as you work so the transfer should be on the heavy side. Replace the pin, adjust the impression and trace the entire design.

Step 7: Slip the carbon paper out from between the tracing and the fabric. Carefully remove all but two of the pins and check your design. Do not remove the pins until you are completely satisfied with your transfer. It is virtually impossible to re-register the transfer once you have removed the pins.

Step 8: When you are satisfied with the transferring process, completely unpin the transfer and gently remove it. You may want to use it for another block, or another quilt.

EMBROIDERING THE BLOCKS

The photographed quilts were made with blocks embroidered following the stitch and color charts which appear on pages 42 to 64 and 81. All stitches are worked with two strands of floss in the needle except French knots which are worked with four. You can, however, use more strands for certain stitches if you wish. Feel free to change stitches or colors.

EMBROIDERED TEDDY BEAR QUILT

What child wouldn't love to snuggle up under this delightful quilt, featuring two appealing little bears spending a busy day—playing in the sand, finger painting, roller skating, baking cookies! Each of the 12 different designs in this quilt is brought to life with easy embroidery stitches and then put together into a delightful quilt.

Size

Approx 42" to 55"

Materials and Equipment

All fabric requirements are based on 44"–45" wide material. If you use narrower-width fabric, adjust yardage accordingly. (Try to get 100% cotton or a blend with no more than 30% synthetic.)

1⅔ yds pale beige (*for blocks*)
⅔ yd solid (*for framing*)
3¼ yds print (*for sashing, borders, binding and backing*)
45" × 60" batting (*crib size; often called "baby batt"*)
Six-strand embroidery floss, 1 skein in each of the following colors
    light, medium and dark brown
    pale, light, medium and dark blue
    light, medium and dark green
    pink
    red
    dark red
    yellow
    gold
    orange
    white
Fabric shears and embroidery scissors
Sewing, embroidery and quilting ("betweens") needles
Sewing and quilting thread (*white is preferred*) or yarn for tying
Beeswax
Embroidery hoop
Quilting hoop or frame
Straight pins
Iron
Tissue or tracing paper
Thimble
Tracing tool

Before cutting, wash and iron all fabrics to be used in the quilt. Make sure that the grain of all fabric is straight and that the fabric is colorfast.

NOTE: The quilt pictured here makes up into a crib quilt, wall hanging or small nap quilt. If you prefer a larger covering suitable for a twin bed, you can alternate embroidered blocks with plain blocks. Plain blocks need no framing, so cut 10½" squares, which will be 10" finished size. You can add decorative quilting on these plain blocks if you desire.

Make 18 embroidered blocks and 17 plain blocks. Set them five across and seven down. You will need to repeat some of the embroidery patterns. Fabric requirements for a twin size (68" × 94") are:

2⅓ yds pale beige (*for embroidered blocks*)
1½ yds print or solid (*for plain blocks*)
2 yds solid (*for framing*)
9 yds print (*for sashing, borders, binding and backing*)
2 skeins embroidery floss in each color

Instructions

Step 1: Cut a piece of pale beige fabric 14" × 14" for each block. Following instructions on page 38, trace the designs.

Step 2: Embroider the blocks. When embroidery is completed, wash block, place face down on a terry towel on ironing board and steam dry. This makes embroidery "stand up". Do not rest the iron on the stitches. Let the steam do the work!

Step 3: Following the instructions for blocking on page 5, block each quilt block to a perfect 8½" square. Cut your cardboard template with a 8½" square opening as in *Fig 1.*

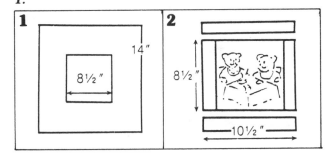

Step 4: From framing fabric cut 24 strips, each 1½" wide and 8½" long and 24 strips, 1½" wide and 10½" long. Frame the blocks as described on page 5 (*Fig 2*).

Step 5: From the sashing fabric, cut nine sashing strips, 3½" wide by 10½" long. Place a sashing strip (**Fig 3: No. 1**) across the bottom of the "Breakfast Time" block, right sides together and stitch. Then sew this same piece of sashing to the top of the "Sandbox Castles" block. In the same manner, stitch the second sashing strip (**Fig 3: No. 2**) to the bottom of the "Sandbox Castles" block and then to the top of the "New Roller Skates" block. Join the third sashing strip (**Fig 3: No. 3**) to bottom of "New Roller Skates" block and to top of "Bedtime Story" block. You now have a vertical strip of four joined blocks. Following **Fig 3** for placement, make two more vertical strips in same manner. You now have three vertical strips, each measuring about 49½" (which includes the ¼" seam allowance at top and bottom). Press all seams to one side before joining the next seam. Cut two sashing strips, each 3½" wide and 49½" long (or the length of your strip of blocks). Sew one strip to each side of the center row of blocks (**Fig 3: Nos. 10 and 11**). Sew the first and third rows of blocks to these same strips, being sure that tops and bottoms of all blocks line up exactly. Press seams.

Step 6: Now complete your quilt top by adding borders of the same fabric to the top, bottom and sides. Cut four border strips, each 3½" wide. Cut two 49½" long (or the length of your quilt top) and two 42½" wide (or the width of your quilt top). In the same manner as for the vertical sashing, sew the two longer border strips to the right and left sides of the quilt top (**Fig 3: Nos. 12 and 13**). Then sew the shorter border strips to the top and bottom (**Fig 3: Nos. 14 and 15**). Give the quilt top a final pressing, making sure all corners are square and that all seams are pressed to one side.

Step 7: Quilt or tie top and attach binding following directions on page 6.

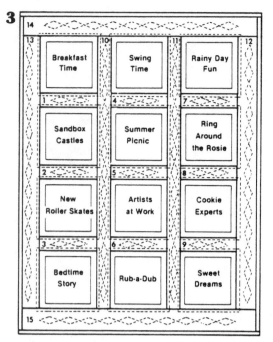

3

Breakfast Time	Swing Time	Rainy Day Fun
Sandbox Castles	Summer Picnic	Ring Around the Rosie
New Roller Skates	Artists at Work	Cookie Experts
Bedtime Story	Rub-a-Dub	Sweet Dreams

Outlines are all worked in stem/outline or straight stitch.

Solid areas are all worked in satin stitch, unless otherwise noted.

Small dots represent French knots (worked with four strands of floss).

In each picture, we worked one bear in light brown with tufts of medium brown; and the other in medium brown, with tufts of dark brown. The satin-stitched nose and tail are worked in the same color as the bear's tufts. All eyes are worked in dark brown satin stitch, and tongues in pink satin stitch. Follow the stitching plans for each individual block for other colors and stitches.

EMBROIDERED FLORAL BOUQUET QUILT

Our most beloved flowers—roses, violets, lilies of the valley, zinnias—all parade in glorious profusion across the blocks of our Floral Bouquet Quilt.

Size

Approx 42" × 55"

Materials and Equipment

All fabric requirements are based on 44"–45" wide material. If you use narrower-width fabric, adjust yardage accordingly. (Try to get 100% cotton or a blend with no more than 30% synthetic.)
1⅔ yds pale beige (*for blocks*)
⅔ yd solid (*for framing*)
3¼ yds print (*for sashing, borders, binding and backing*)
45" × 60" batting (*crib size; often called "baby batt"*)
Six-strand embroidery floss, 1 skein in each of the following colors
    light, medium and dark pink
    light and medium yellow-green
    light, medium and dark green
    light, medium and dark blue
    light, medium and dark purple
    light, medium and dark orange
    light and medium gray
    yellow
    gold
    white
Fabric shears and embroidery scissors
Sewing, embroidery and quilting ("betweens") needles
Sewing and quilting thread (*white is preferred*) or yarn for tying
Beeswax
Embroidery hoop
Quilting hoop or frame
Straight pins
Iron
Tissue or tracing paper
Thimble
Tracing tool

Before cutting, wash and iron all fabrics to be used in the quilt. Make sure that the grain of all fabric is straight and that the fabric is colorfast.

NOTE: The quilt pictured here makes up into a crib quilt, wall hanging or small nap quilt. If you prefer a larger covering suitable for a twin bed, you can alternate embroi-

dered blocks with plain blocks. Plain blocks need no framing, so cut 10½" squares, which will be 10" finished size. You can add decorative quilting on these plain squares, if you desire.

Make 18 embroidered blocks and 17 plain blocks. Set them five across and seven down. You will need to repeat some of the embroidery patterns. Fabric requirements for a twin size (68" × 94") are:

2⅓ yds pale beige *(for embroidered blocks)*
1½ yds print or solid *(for plain blocks)*
2 yds solid *(for framing)*
9 yds print *(for sashing, borders, binding and backing)*
2 skeins embroidery floss in each color

Instructions

Step 1: Cut a piece of pale beige fabric 14" × 14" for each block. Following instructions on page 38, trace the designs.

Step 2: Embroider the blocks. When embroidery is completed, wash block, place face down on a terry towel on ironing board and steam dry. This makes embroidery "stand up". Do not rest the iron on the stitches. Let the steam do the work!

Step 3: Following the instructions for blocking on page 5, block each quilt block to a perfect 8½" square. Cut your cardboard template with a 8½" square opening as in *Fig 1*, page 39.

Step 4: From framing fabric cut 24 strips, each 1½" wide and 8½" long and 24 strips, 1½" wide and 10½" long. Frame the blocks as described on page 5, and *Fig 2*, page 39.

Step 5: From the sashing fabric, cut nine sashing strips, 3½" wide by 10½" long. Place a sashing strip (*Fig 1: No. 1*) across the bottom of the "Wild Roses" block, right sides together and stitch. Then sew this same piece of sashing to the top of the "Violets" block. In the same manner, stitch the second sashing strip (*Fig 1: No. 2*) to the bottom of the "Violets" block and then to the top of the "Daisies" block.

Join the third sashing strip (*Fig 1: No. 3*) to bottom of "Daisies" block and to top of "Forget-Me-Nots" block. You now have a vertical strip of four joined blocks. Following *Fig 1* for placement, make two more vertical strips in same manner. You now have three vertical strips, each measuring about 49½" (which includes the ¼" seam allowance at top and bottom). Press all seams to one side before joining the next seam. Cut two sashing strips, each 3½" wide and 49½" long (or the length of your strip of blocks). Sew one strip to each side of the center row of blocks (*Fig 1: Nos. 10 and 11*). Sew the first and third rows of blocks to these same strips, being sure that tops and bottoms of all blocks line up exactly. Press seams.

Step 6: Now complete your quilt top by adding borders of the same fabric to the top, bottom and sides. Cut four border strips, each 3½" wide. Cut two 49½" long (or the length of your quilt top) and two 42½" wide (or the width of your quilt top). In the same manner as for the vertical sashing, sew the two longer border strips to the right and left sides of the quilt top (*Fig 1: Nos. 12 and 13*). Then sew the shorter border strips to the top and bottom (*Fig. 1: Nos. 14 and 15*). Give the quilt top a final pressing, making sure all corners are square and that all seams are pressed to one side.

Step 7: Quilt or tie top and attach binding following directions on page 6.

Outlines are all worked in stem/outline or straight stitch.

Small dots represent French knots (worked with four strands of floss).

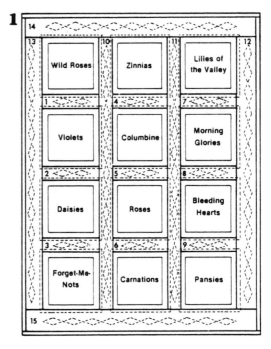

Ribbons are worked in chain stitch.

Leaves are all worked in outline stitch with straight stitches on the inside unless otherwise noted.

Stems are all worked in two rows of outline stitch.

Where three or four colors are indicated for a flower, work from light to dark for shading.

Follow the stitching plans for each individual block for other colors and stitches.

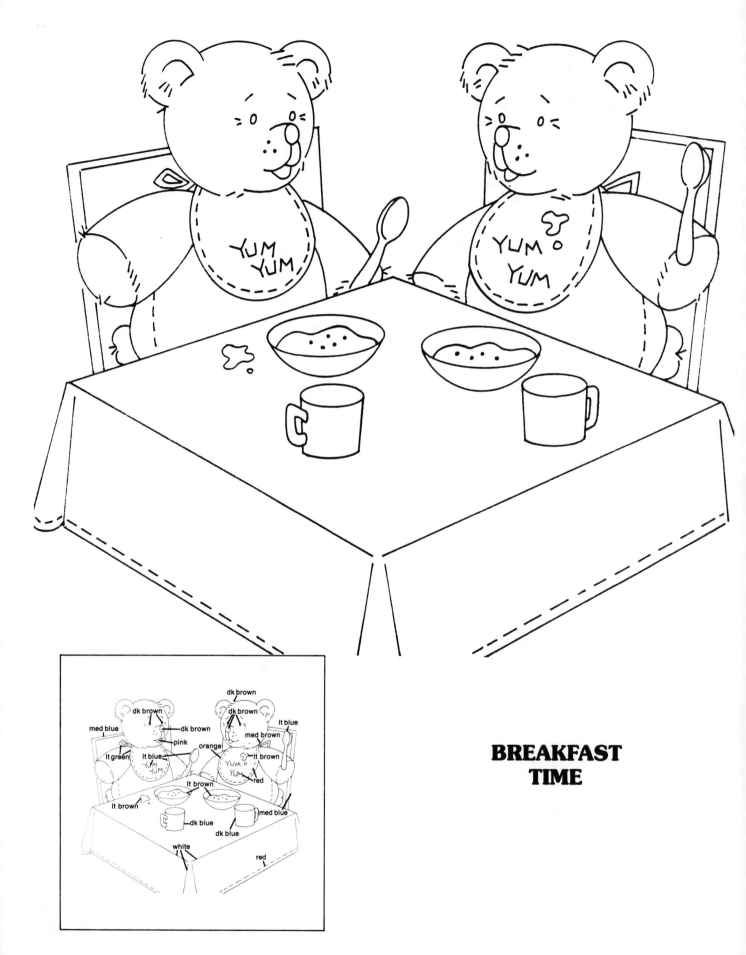

**BREAKFAST
TIME**

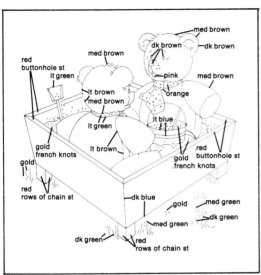

SANDBOX CASTLES

NEW
ROLLER
SKATES

BEDTIME
STORY

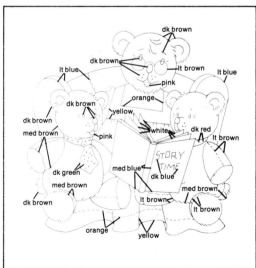

SWINGTIME

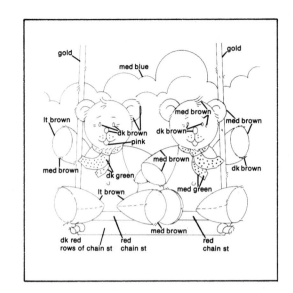

SUMMER
PICNIC

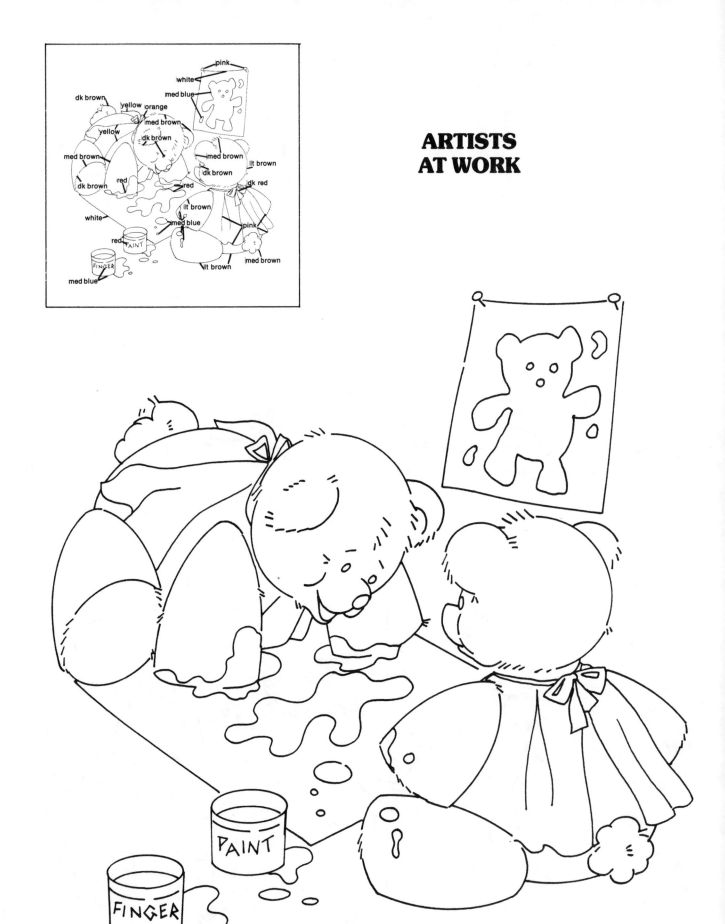

ARTISTS
AT WORK

48

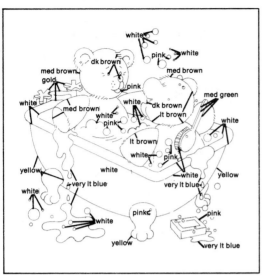

RUB-A-
DUB-DUB

49

RAINY DAY
FUN

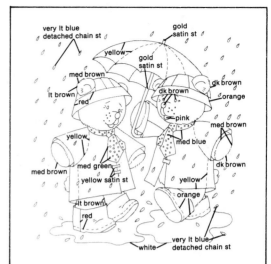

50

RING
AROUND
THE ROSIE

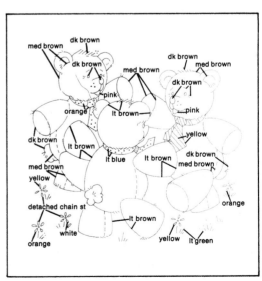

COOKIE
EXPERTS

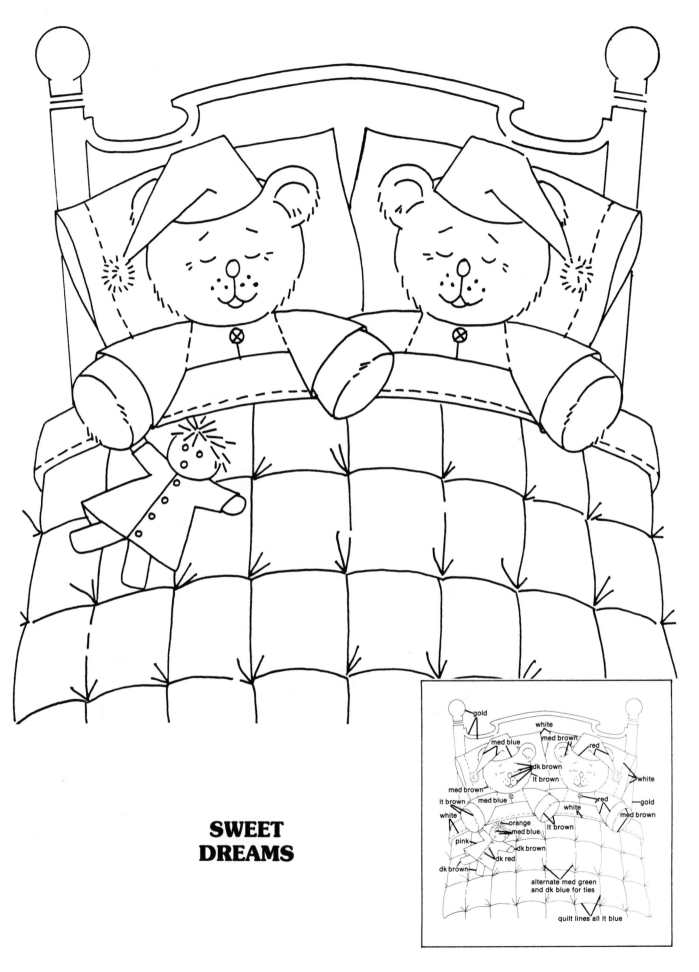

**SWEET
DREAMS**

gold

white

med brown

med blue

red

dk brown

lt brown

med brown

white

lt brown

med blue

gold

white

white

med brown

orange

med blue

lt brown

pink

dk brown

dk red

dk brown

alternate med green
and dk blue for ties

quilt lines all lt blue

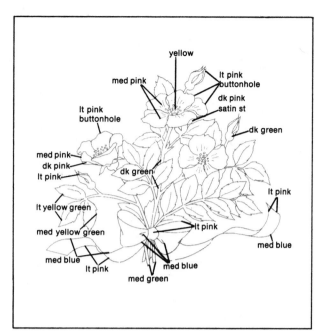

WILD
ROSES

54

VIOLETS

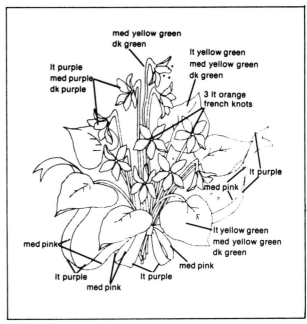

med yellow green
dk green

lt yellow green
med yellow green
dk green

lt purple
med purple
dk purple

3 lt orange
french knots

lt purple

med pink

lt yellow green
med yellow green
dk green

med pink

med pink

lt purple

med pink

lt purple

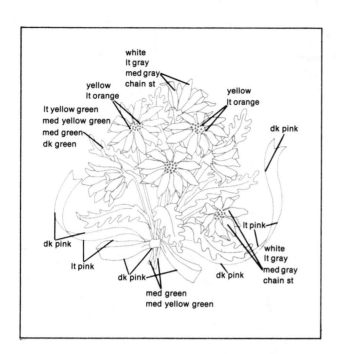

DAISIES

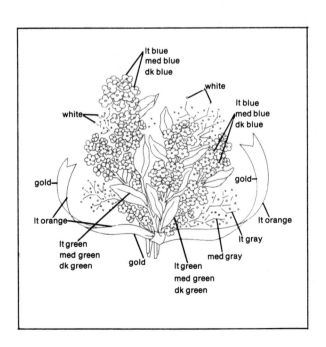

FORGET-ME-NOTS

ZINNIAS

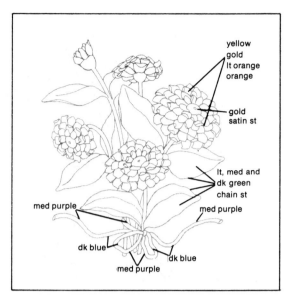

yellow
gold
lt orange
orange

gold
satin st

lt, med and
dk green
chain st

med purple

med purple

dk blue

dk blue

med purple

58

COLUMBINE

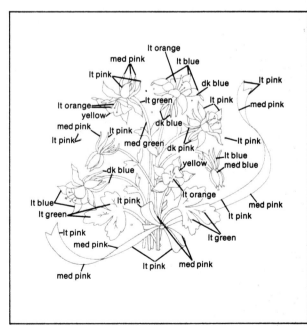

ROSES

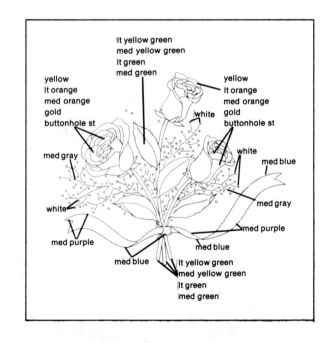

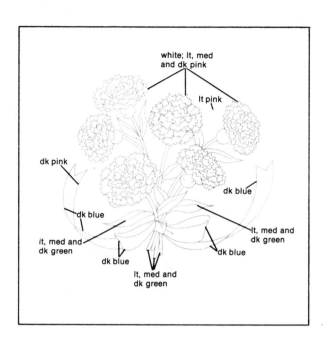

CARNATIONS

LILLIES
OF THE
VALLEY

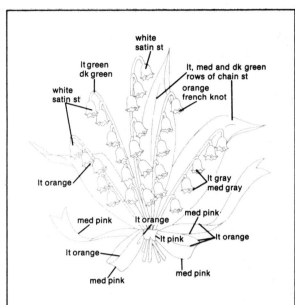

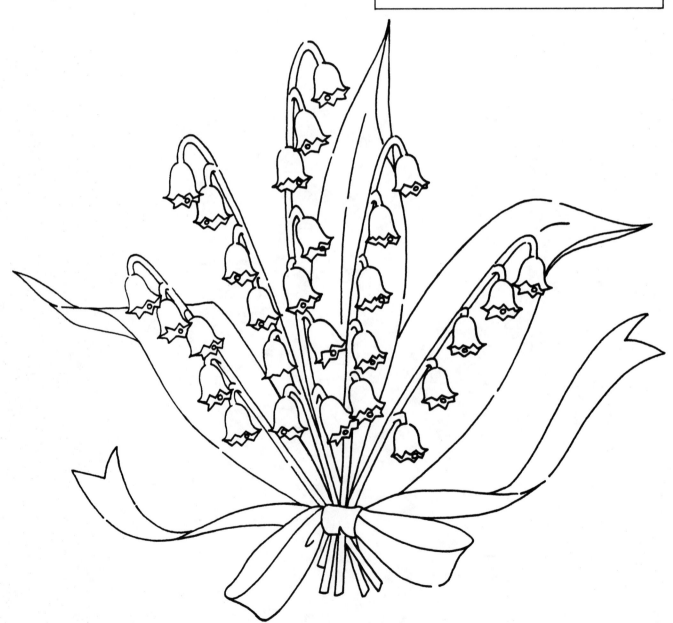

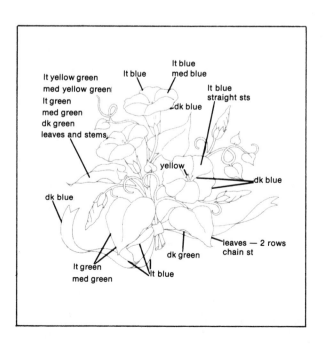

lt yellow green
med yellow green
lt green
med green
dk green
leaves and stems

lt blue

lt blue
med blue

lt blue
straight sts

dk blue

yellow

dk blue

dk blue

lt green
med green

lt blue

dk green

leaves — 2 rows
chain st

MORNING GLORIES

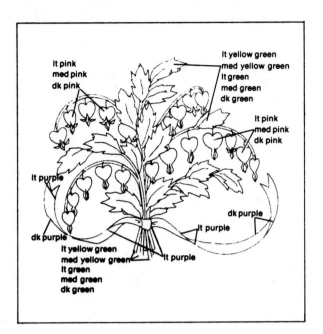

BLEEDING
HEARTS

Embroidery patterns for FLORAL BOUQUET QUILT continue on page 81.

CANDLEWICK CRIB QUILT

DETAIL

EARLY AMERICAN STENCIL QUILT

PRESIDENT'S WREATH

ROSE OF SHARON

PRAIRIE FLOWER

OHIO ROSE

EMBROIDERED TEDDY BEAR QUILT

PAINTED TEDDY BEAR QUILT

LACE NET SAMPLER QUILT

DETAIL

LACE NET CRIB QUILT

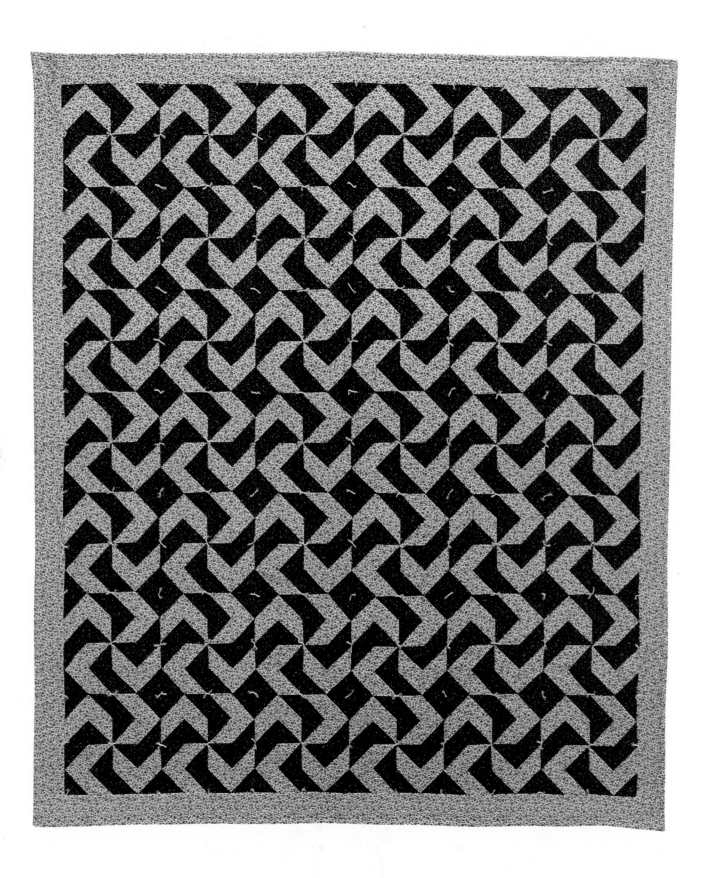

FLYFOOT SEWING MACHINE QUILT

CARD TRICKS SEWING MACHINE QUILT

PLANTING

WATERING

RAKING

BLOOMING

74

CHICKEN SCRATCH™ QUILT

PAINTED FLORAL BOUQUET QUILT

CANDLEWICK SUNBONNET SUE QUILT

(Continued from page 64)

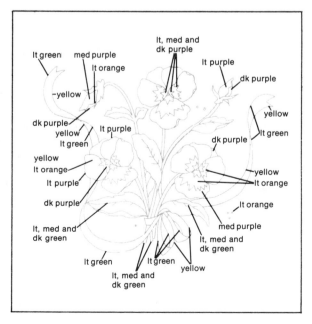

PANSIES

Painted Quilts

If the only craft you feel at home with is coloring in a child's coloring book, you can still make a beautiful quilt. Transfer these designs to fabric and then color inside the lines with fabric paints or markers. What fun!

PAINTING HOW-TO

THE FABRIC

Use a good quality 100% cotton in a pale color, such as a beige for your quilt blocks. Before transferring your design, wash the fabric in hot water to remove sizing and to prevent any further shrinkage. If you have difficulty locating a 100% cotton in your color choice, you can use a blend, but try to find one that has no more than 30% synthetic fibers. Before making your final choice of fabric, test your paints to find the fabric that works the best.

THE PAINT

Check at your local craft store or department for fabric paints. Any good quality fabric paint will be satisfactory. Paints are also marketed in ball point tubes especially for painting on fabric. These are easy to work with since you treat them exactly like a pencil; they make sharp outlines and can be blended for shading or to make additional colors. In addition some felt-tipped markers are colorfast and can be used. **Before using any paint, we suggest that you do a washability test!**

OTHER SUPPLIES

A blotter placed under the fabric while you are painting is helpful. A metal embroidery hoop with a hard blotter-covered center is the perfect surface for painting on fabric. It holds the work smooth and taut assuring uniform results with no fuzzy edges.

TRANSFERRING THE DESIGNS

Follow the instructions on page 38.

PAINTING THE BLOCKS

For color suggestions, you may want to study the color and stitch charts on pages 42 to 64 and 81, follow the color photographs on pages 69 and 78, or use your own imagination. Follow the manufacturer's instructions for using your choice of paints. When the block is completely dry, press following manufacturer's instructions to render block colorfast.

PAINTED TEDDY BEAR QUILT

Our two bears are especially delightful when rendered in bright colors. No child could resist taking a nap when he's cuddling up under this charming quilt.

Size

Approx 42″ × 55″

Materials and Equipment

All fabric requirements are based on 44″–45″ wide material. If you use narrower-width fabric, adjust yardage accordingly.
1⅔ yds pale beige (for blocks)
⅔ yd solid (for framing)

3¼ yds print (for sashing, borders, binding and backing)
45″ × 60″ batting (crib size; often called "Baby Batt")
Fabric paints in your choice of colors; some suggestions are listed below:

    light, medium and dark brown
    pale, light, medium and dark blue
    light, medium and dark green
    pink
    red and dark red
    yellow
    gold
    orange
    white

NOTE: The quilt pictured here makes up into a crib quilt, wall hanging or small nap quilt. If you prefer a larger covering suitable for a twin bed, you can alternate painted blocks with plain blocks. Plain blocks need no framing, so cut 10½" squares which will be 10" finished size. You can add decorative quilting on these plain blocks if you desire.

Make 18 painted blocks and 17 plain blocks. Set them five across and seven down. You will need to repeat some of the painted patterns. Fabric requirements for a twin size (68" × 94") are:

2⅓ yds pale beige (*for painted blocks*)
1½ yds print or solid (*for plain blocks*)
2 yds solid (*for framing*)
9 yds print (*for sashing, borders, binding and backing*)

Instructions

Step 1: Cut a piece of pale beige fabric 14" × 14" for each block. Following instructions on page 38, trace the designs.

Step 2: Paint the blocks. When painting is completed, follow manufacturer's instructions for making block colorfast.

Step 3: Following instructions for blocking on page 5, block each quilt block to a perfect 8½" square. Cut your cardboard template with an 8½" square opening as in *Fig 1*, page 39.

Step 4: From framing fabric cut 24 strips, each 1½" wide and 8½" long and 24 strips, 1½" wide and 10½" long. Frame the blocks as described on page 5 and *Fig 2*, page 39.

Step 5: Follow step 5 under Embroidered Teddy Bear Quilt on page 40.

Step 6: Follow step 6 under Embroidered Teddy Bear Quilt on page 40.

Step 7: Quilt or tie top and attach binding following directions on page 6.

Brushes
Fabric shears
Sewing and quilting ("betweens") needles
Sewing and quilting thread (*white is preferred*) or yarn
   for tying
Beeswax
Embroidery hoop and blotter
Quilting hoop or frame
Straight pins
Iron
Tissue or tracing paper
Tracing Tool
Thimble

Before cutting, wash and iron all fabrics to be used in the quilt. Make sure that the grain of all fabric is straight and that the fabric is colorfast.

PAINTED FLORAL BOUQUET QUILT

Paint a beautiful bouquet of roses, violets, lillies of the valley, or zinnias. Then put the bouquets together to create a magnificent Floral Bouquet Quilt. If you think you have just created a masterpiece, why not hang it on the wall like a beautiful painting.

Size

Approx 42" × 55"

Materials and Equipment

All fabric requirements are based on 44"–45" wide material. If you use narrower-width fabric, adjust yardage accordingly.
1⅔ yds pale beige (*for blocks*)
⅔ yd solid (*for framing*)

3¼ yds print (*for sashing, borders, binding and backing*)
45" × 60" batting (*crib size; often called "baby batt"*)
Fabric paints in your choice of colors; some suggestions
   are listed below:
      light, medium and dark pink
      light and medium yellow-green
      light, medium and dark green
      light, medium and dark blue
      light, medium and dark purple
      light, medium and dark orange
      light and medium gray
      yellow
      gold
      white
Brushes
Fabric shears

Sewing and quilting ("betweens") needles

Sewing and quilting thread (*white is preferred*) or yarn for tying

Beeswax

Embroidery hoop and blotter

Quilting hoop or frame

Straight pins

Iron

Tissue or tracing paper

Tracing tool

Thimble

Before cutting, wash and iron all fabrics to be used in the quilt. Make sure that the grain of all fabric is straight and that the fabric is colorfast.

NOTE: The quilt pictured here makes up into a crib quilt, wall hanging or small nap quilt. If you prefer a larger covering suitable for a twin bed, you can alternate painted blocks with plain blocks. Plain blocks need no framing, so cut 10½" squares which will be 10" finished size. You can decorate the plain blocks with decorative quilting if you desire.

Make 18 painted blocks and 17 plain blocks. Set them five across and seven down. You will need to repeat some of the painted patterns. Fabric requirements for a twin size (68" × 94") are:

2⅓ yds pale beige (*for painted blocks*)

1½ yds print or solid (*for plain blocks*)

2 yds solid (*for framing*)

9 yds print (*for sashing, borders, binding and backing*)

Instructions

Step 1: Cut a piece of pale beige fabric 14" × 14" for each block. Following instructions on page 38, trace the designs.

Step 2: Paint the blocks. When painting is completed, follow manufacturer's instructions for making block colorfast.

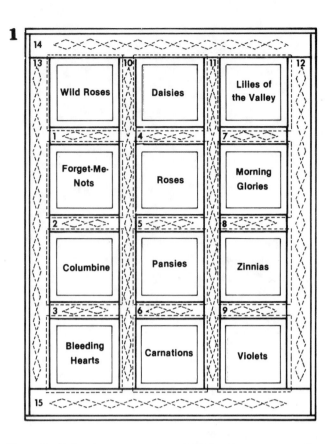

Step 3: Following instructions for blocking on page 5, block each quilt block to a perfect 8½" square. Cut your cardboard template with an 8½" square opening as in *Fig 1*, page 39.

Step 4: From framing fabric cut 24 strips, each 1½" wide and 8½" long and 24 strips, 1½" wide and 10½" long. Frame the blocks as described on page 5 and *Fig 2*, page 39.

Step 5: From the sashing fabric, cut nine sashing strips, 3½" wide by 10½" long. Place a sashing strip (*Fig 1: No. 1*) across the bottom of the "Wild Roses" block, right sides together and stitch. Then sew this same piece of sashing to the top of the "Forget-Me-Nots" block. In the same manner, stitch the second sashing strip (*Fig 1: No. 2*) to the bottom of the "Forget-Me-Nots" block and then to the top of the "Columbine" block. Join the third sashing strip (*Fig 1: No. 3*) to the bottom of the "Columbine" block and to the top of the "Bleeding Hearts" block. You now have a vertical strip of four joined blocks. Following Fig 3 for placement, make two more vertical strips in same manner. You now have three vertical strips, each measuring about 49½" (which includes the ¼" seam allowance at top and bottom). Press all seams to one side before joining the next seam. Cut two sashing strips, each 3½" wide and 49½" long (or the length of your strip of blocks). Sew one strip to each side of the center row of blocks (*Fig 1: Nos. 10 and 11*). Sew the first and third rows of blocks to these same strips, being sure that tops and bottoms of all blocks line up exactly. Press seams.

Step 6: Follow step 6 under Embroidered Floral Bouquet Quilt on page 41.

Step 7: Quilt or tie top and attach binding following directions on page 6.

Candlewicking

Candlewicking!

Ah, the very name conjures up the picture of our Colonial ancestor saving her tiny bits of candlewick thread, left over from her day's candlemaking, and from these bits creating beautiful counterpanes.

Sounds very romantic, but unfortunately it isn't true. The name derives from an old embroidery technique that used the soft-spun thread that was also used for making wicks for candles. After the embroidery was completed, the fabric was washed in very hot water. This caused the stitches to fluff up, and the fabric to shrink, thereby holding the stitches in place.

Now with the renewed interest in our heritage, the art of Candlewicking has returned. Unfortunately, modern technology has left us with fabrics that barely shrink and threads that no longer fluff. We can still, however, create beautiful heirlooms using modern embroidery stitches, and we use the hot water bath to shrink the fabric just slightly so that it produces the soft wrinkled look of old-time Candlewicking.

CANDLEWICKING HOW-TO

THE FABRIC

Candlewicking is usually done on 100% cotton un-bleached muslin, which has *not* been preshrunk. Do not wash fabric for Candlewicking before stitching on it. The fabric is washed after stitching; the shrinkage will not only hold the knots, but it will also give the project the puckered look of traditional Candlewicking. If you prefer less shrinkage, purchase a good quality 100% cotton, which will shrink only about 2% to 3%. If you like the puckered look, buy a fabric which will give you an 8% to 10% shrinkage. The quilts photographed in this book were made on fabric with a minimum of shrinkage.

THE THREAD

We have used a special Candlewicking thread for the quilts in this book. This is a 100% cotton thread with four plies. The plies can be separated and used in different combinations. We have used both colored and all-white Candlewicking thread. If Candlewicking thread is not available in a color of your choice, you can substitute other threads such as embroidery floss (approximately twelve strands will give you the same effect as Candlewicking thread), pearl cotton, crochet cotton, cotton knit and crochet yarn, darning yarn—even kite twine. Because threads differ in thickness, experiment until you achieve the desired effect.

You may wish to use only one strand, or more than 20, depending upon the individual thread.

NOTE: Test all colored Candlewick thread for color-fastness by washing in hot water.

THE NEEDLES

You'll need a sharp, long-eyed needle, such as a #2 Crewel Needle or a #20 Chenille Needle. Or, look for packets of needles called "Candlewicking Assortment".

THE HOOPS

Stretch the fabric in an embroidery hoop or small frame. Keep the fabric taut for easier stitching. The use of a floor stand frees both hands and makes stitching easier.

THE STITCHES

Traditional embroidery stitches—French Knots, Stem/Outline, Satin and Padded Satin are used in our quilts. One stitch that may be new to you is the Colonial Knot, which is a simple variation of the French Knot. All of the stitches, except the Colonial Knot, are worked with 2 strands of Candlewicking thread. We suggest that you cut the thread twice the stitching length desired (about 36"), thread it into the needle, bring ends together and make a knot. This gives you an 18" stitching length. Working this way, rather than using 2 individual 18″ strands gives an even tension and, because there is less bulk near the eye, makes it easier to pull the thread through the fabric.

The Colonial Knot is worked with 4 strands. Cut 2 strands about 36″ long, and thread into needle. Bring all 4 ends together and knot. Candlewicking is one of the few embroidery techniques in which knots can be used to start a new thread. To end off, run the needle back through an inch or so of stitching.

To keep the embroidery hoop from crushing the French and Colonial Knots, stitch them last. You can begin stitching in any area of the design, but avoid long jumps from one area to another; the thread across the back of the work will leave shadows.

Following are instructions for working the stitches used in our Candlewick quilts:

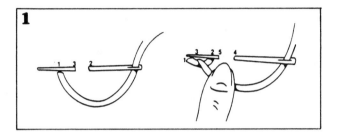

STEM/OUTLINE (worked with 2 strands): In the figures, needle comes up through work at 1 and all odd numbers, down through fabric at 2 and all even numbers. Keep thread below needle at all times. At point 5, bring needle up and from now on always bring needle up through a previously used hole. Continue in this manner (*Fig 1*).

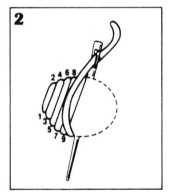

SATIN (worked with 2 strands): In the figure, needle comes up through work at 1 and all odd numbers, down at 2 and all even numbers. Keep tension even and the strands of thread smooth (*Fig 2*).

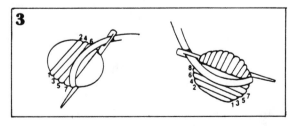

PADDED SATIN (worked with 2 strands): To give added dimension to the stitch, the traditional Satin Stitch is

worked over a foundation of padding stitches. First work the padding, taking long stitches within the area outline, placed so they slant in the opposite direction in which the top Satin Stitches will go. Bring needle up at 1 and all odd stitches, down at 2 and all even stitches (*Fig 3*).

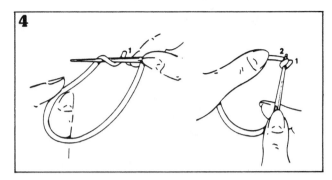

FRENCH KNOTS (worked with 2 strands): Bring needle up at 1, hold thread close to work with left thumb and index finger. Slip needle under thread, and turn needle clockwise. Still holding thread in left fingers, insert needle back down through fabric at 2, maintaining firm tension on thread until it is almost completely down through the fabric (*Fig 4*).

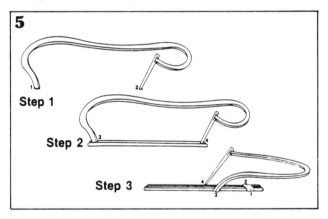

COUCHING (worked with 2 strands): In couching, thread strands are laid on top of the fabric, then tied down with small stitches. For added texture, we worked our Couching Stitches with 4 strands, laid 2 strands at a time to ensure their lying flat. In **Step 1**, bring needle up at 1 and down at 2: you have now laid 2 threads; in **Step 2**, bring needle up at 3 (*between* the 2 strands laid down in Step 1); then back down again at 4, again between the first 2 strands. Now secure the 4 laid threads with small tie-down Couching Stitches as in **Step 3**, angling stitches slightly to the left. Bring needle up at 1 and down at 2; then up at 3 and down at 4. Continue in same manner across laid area, spacing the tie-down stitches about ¼″ apart. Take care not to pull the tie-down stitches too tightly. This method gives an attractive raised rope effect (*Fig 5*).

COLONIAL KNOTS (worked with 4 strands): Step 1: Bring needle up through fabric at 1, then hold thread firmly with left thumb and index finger about 2″ from point 1. Hold threaded needle in right hand as you would hold a pencil and cross over left hand so needle goes under the thread from left side (*Fig 6*). This is an awkward step and does take some practice before it becomes a comfortable

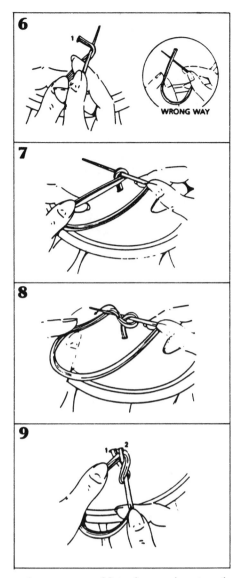

and natural movement. Note figure showing the wrong way.

Step 2: Continue to hold thread firmly with left thumb and index finger and turn needle to left (from vertical to horizontal position), which loops thread around needle. (**Fig 7**).

Step 3: With left hand bring thread up and over needle (**Fig 8**). The thread now forms a figure 8.

Step 4: Turn needle back to vertical position and insert it down through fabric at 2. Continuing to hold thread firmly with left hand, pull needle and thread down through fabric, giving left hand thread a firm tug just before thread is pulled completely through (**Fig 9**). This assures a tight, firm knot.

TRANSFERRING THE DESIGNS

The Candlewick designs for each of the blocks for the Candlewick quilts appear on pages 91 to 114 and 116.

Step 1: Do not prewash fabric before Candlewicking. Iron the block so that it is smooth. Find center of your fabric by folding it in half vertically and horizontally. Mark center.

Step 2: Open book to desired pattern and lay book flat. A piece of white paper or cardboard placed under page will be a help in seeing pattern clearly.

Step 3: Find center of your design. Note that there are arrows at top, bottom and along sides of each of the designs. The meeting place of these lines is center of design. Match center of design with center of fabric. Lay fabric over design and tape down.

Step 4: With a water-soluble marking pen, trace pattern. (*NOTE: Test all water-soluble pens before using to make absolutely sure that the dots will wash out. Never trust manufacturer's statement.*) The dot should wash out cleanly without leaving any residue on fabric or thread.

CANDLEWICKING THE BLOCKS

The stitch charts accompanying the quilts show what stitches we used in our quilts. In addition, we tell which colors we used in our colored quilt. Feel free to substitute stitches and colors as you choose; if we show an area worked with Satin, you might prefer to fill it with Colonial Knots, or leave it open and work Stem/Outline around it.

WASHING THE CANDLEWICKING

In traditional Candlewicking, washing the completed embroidery in very hot water was the final step. This caused the fabric to shrink, and the stitches to stand up. Today the hot water bath will cause the fabric to shrink slightly, giving the work the soft, puckered look of antique Candlewicking.

Before attempting the hot water bath, wash Candlewicking in cold water to remove all traces of marking pen. Make sure that there are no blue lines hiding in fabric to haunt you later. If fabric is very soiled, you may wish to use a mild soap.

Now wash your Candlewicking in very hot water to cause the fabric to shrink as described above. Roll fabric in soft terry towel to eliminate moisture. Unroll and place stitched piece face down on a dry terry towel on ironing board and steam until dry. This will make embroidery "stand up". Do not let the steam iron rest on the stitches; the steam does the work!

CANDLEWICK SAMPLER QUILT

While Candlewicking today is being used to decorate pillows and other items, it is most appropriate to use this technique for its original purpose—a cover for the bed. All of the designs in this sampler quilt are based upon quilting patterns, one of the traditional sources for Candlewick designs. If you wish, you can use these designs to make pillows or other projects as shown in the photo.

Size

Approx 51″ × 67″

Materials and Equipment

All fabric requirements are based on 44″–45″ wide material. If you are using narrower fabric, adjust yardage accordingly.

1⅔ yds unbleached muslin (*for blocks*)
(*NOTE: Use a good quality 100% cotton which has not been preshrunk.*)
16 yds 2″ ecru insertion lace (*for framing*)
3 yds natural-color cotton (*for framing, sashing, borders and binding*)
4 yds fabric (*for backing*)
(*NOTE: Unbleached muslin can be used for backing. Be sure to shrink this muslin before cutting.*)
1 package twin size quilt batting
250 yds Candlewicking thread
Fabric shears and embroidery scissors
Sewing, candlewicking and quilting needles
Sewing and quilting thread (*white is preferred*)
Beeswax
Embroidery hoop
Quilting hoop or frame
Straight pins
Iron
Thimble
Tissue or tracing paper
Water-soluble marking pen

Before cutting, wash and iron fabrics to be used for sashing, framing, borders, binding and backing. **Do not prewash fabric to be used for candlewick blocks.** Make sure that the grain of all fabric is straight.

Instructions

Step 1: Cut a piece of Candlewick fabric 14″ × 14″ for each block. Following instructions on page 87, trace the designs.

Step 2: Candlewick the blocks.

Step 3: Following the instructions on page 87, wash the blocks in cold and hot water.

Step 4: Following the instructions for blocking on page 5, block each quilt block to a perfect 10½″ square. Cut your cardboard template with a 10½″ square opening as in **Fig 1**.

Step 5: The framing for the blocks is made up of insertion lace mounted on a strip of fabric. From the framing fabric cut 24 strips, each 2″ wide and 10½″ long and 24 strips, 2″ wide and 13½″ long. Now cut 24 strips of matching in-

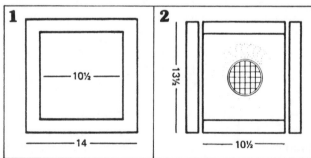

sertion lace, each 10½″ long and 24 strips, 13½″ long. Right sides up, place insertion lace **over** framing fabric and pin. Work with lace and framing fabric as one. Frame the blocks as described on page 5 (**Fig 2**).

Step 6: From sashing fabric cut nine sashing strips, 3½″ wide by 13½″ long. Making sure top of each design is in right position, place sashing strip (**Fig 3: No. 1**) across bottom of "Bridal Wreath" block right sides together and stitch. Then sew same piece of sashing to top of "Double Wedding Ring" block. In same manner stitch second sashing strip (**Fig 3: No. 2**) to bottom of "Double Wedding Ring" block and then to top of "Feather Circle" block. Join third sashing strip (**Fig 3: No. 3**) to bottom of "Feather

3

14			
13	**10**	**11**	**12**
Bridal Wreath	Roses and Tulips	Rose and Fan	
1	**4**	**7**	
Double Wedding Ring	Butterfly	Tulips	
2	**5**	**8**	
Feather Circle	Prairie Flower	Feather	
3	**6**	**9**	
Rose of Sharon	President's Wreath	Roses	
15			

Circle" block and to top of "Rose of Sharon" block. You now have a vertical strip of four joined blocks. Following Fig 3 for placement, make two more vertical strips in same manner. You now have three vertical strips each measuring about 61½" (which includes ¼" seam allowance at top and bottom). Press all seams to one side before joining next seam.

Step 7: Cut two sashing strips, each 3½" wide and 61½" long (or length of your strip of blocks). Sew one strip to each side of center row of blocks (**Fig 3: Nos. 10 and 11**). Sew first and third rows of blocks to these same strips, being sure that tops and bottoms of all blocks line up exactly. Press seams.

Step 8: Now complete quilt top by adding borders to top, bottom and sides. Cut four border strips, each 3½" wide. Cut two 61½" long (or length of your quilt top) and two 51½" wide (or width of your quilt top). In same manner as for vertical sashing, sew two longer border strips to right and left sides of quilt top (**Fig 3: Nos. 12 and 13**). Then sew shorter border strips to top and bottom (**Fig 3: Nos. 14 and 15**). Give quilt top final steaming, making sure all corners are square and that all seams are pressed to one side.

Step 9: Quilt or tie top and attach binding following directions on page 6.

Designs and stitch charts appear on pages 91-102.

CANDLEWICK CRIB QUILTS

What warmer welcome could there be for the new baby than a delightful old-fashioned baby quilt! Here are 12 charming designs sure to bring a smile to both baby and the new mother. We show the designs combined in a traditional white-on-white quilt and in a quilt worked in colored Candlewick threads. The choice is yours. Work all 12 blocks in one quilt, or try a quilt made entirely with one block repeated 12 times.

Size
Approx 42" × 55

Materials and Equipment (for each Quilt)
All fabric requirements are based on 44"–45" wide material. If you are using narrower fabric, adjust yardage accordingly.

1⅔ yds unbleached muslin (*for blocks*) (*NOTE: Use a good quality 100% cotton which has not been preshrunk.*)
13 yds 1½" ecru insertion lace (*for framing*)
3 yds natural-color cotton (*for framing, sashing, borders and binding*)
2 yds fabric (*for backing*)
1 package crib size quilt batting
200 yds natural Candlewicking thread (*for natural quilt*)
one 50 yd card of **each** of the following colors (*for colored quilt*):

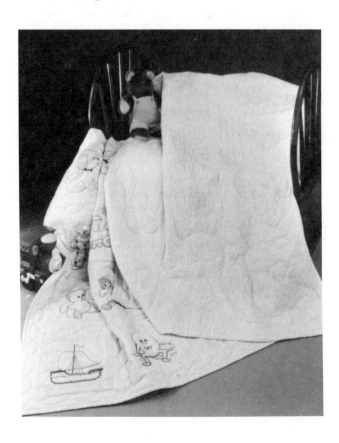

pink	gold	orange
red	light green	lavender
rust	dark green	royal blue
yellow		

Fabric shears and embroidery scissors
Sewing, Candlewicking and quilting needles
Sewing and quilting thread (*white is preferred*)

Beeswax	Iron
Embroidery hoop	Thimble
Quilting hoop	Tissue or tracing paper
Straight pins	Water-soluble marking pen

Before cutting, wash and iron fabrics to be used for sashing, framing, borders, binding and backing. **Do not pre-wash fabric to be used for Candlewick blocks**. Make sure that the grain of all fabric is straight.

Instructions

Step 1: Cut a piece of Candlewick fabric 14″ × 14″ for each block. Follow instructions on page 87 and trace designs.

Step 2: Candlewick the blocks.

Step 3: Following instructions on page 87, wash blocks in cold and hot water.

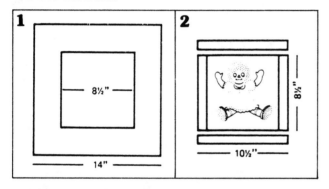

Step 4: Following instructions for blocking on page 5, block each quilt block to a perfect 8½″ square. Cut your cardboard template with an 8½″ square opening as in *Fig 1*.

Step 5: The framing for the blocks is made up of insertion lace mounted on a strip of fabric. From the framing fabric cut 24 strips, each 1½″ wide and 8½″ long and 24 strips, 1½″ wide and 10½″ long. Now cut 24 strips of matching insertion lace each 8½″ long and 24 strips, 10½″ long. Right sides up, lay insertion lace over framing fabric and pin. Work with lace and framing as one. Frame the blocks as described on page 5 (*Fig 2*).

Step 6: From sashing fabric, cut nine sashing strips 3½″ wide by 10½″ long.

NOTE: Be sure the top of each design is in the right position. Place sashing strip (*Fig 3: No. 1*) across bottom of "Doggy" block right sides together and stitch. Then sew same piece of sashing to top of "Clown" block. In same manner stitch second sashing strip (*Fig 3: No. 2*) to bottom of "Clown" block and then to top of "Teddy" block. Join third sashing strip (*Fig 3: No. 3*) to bottom of "Teddy" block and to top of "Sail Boat" block. You now have a vertical strip of four joined blocks. Following *Fig 3* for placement, make two more vertical strips in same manner. You now have three vertical strips each measur-

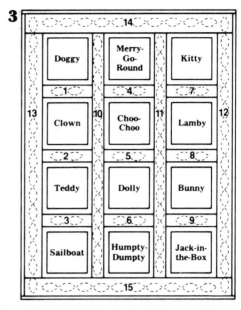

ing about 49½″ (which includes ¼″ seam allowance at top and bottom). Press all seams to one side before joining next seam. Cut two sashing strips, each 3½″ wide and 49½″ long (or length of your strip of blocks). Sew one strip to each side of center row of blocks (*Fig 3: Nos. 10 and 11*). Sew first and third rows of blocks to these same strips, being sure that tops and bottoms of all blocks line up exactly. Press seams.

Step 8: Now complete quilt top by adding borders to top, bottom and sides. Cut four border strips, each 3½″ wide. Cut two 49½″ long (or length of your quilt top) and two 42½″ wide (or width of your quilt top). In same manner as for vertical sashing, sew two longer border strips to right and left sides of quilt top (*Fig 3: Nos. 12 and 13*). Then sew shorter border strips to top and bottom (*Fig 3: Nos. 14 and 15*). Give quilt top final steaming, making sure all corners are square and that all seams are pressed to one side.

Step 9: Quilt or tie top and attach binding following directions on page 6.

Designs and stitch/color charts appear on pages 103-114.

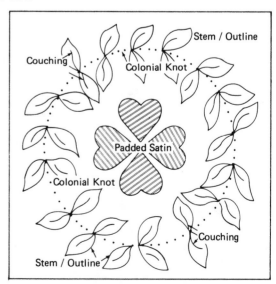

BRIDAL WREATH

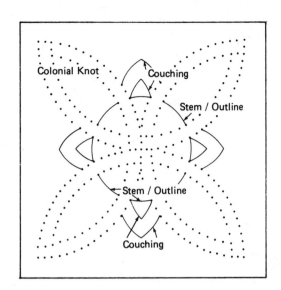

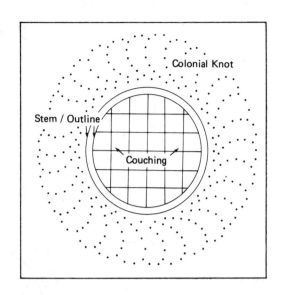

DOUBLE WEDDING RING

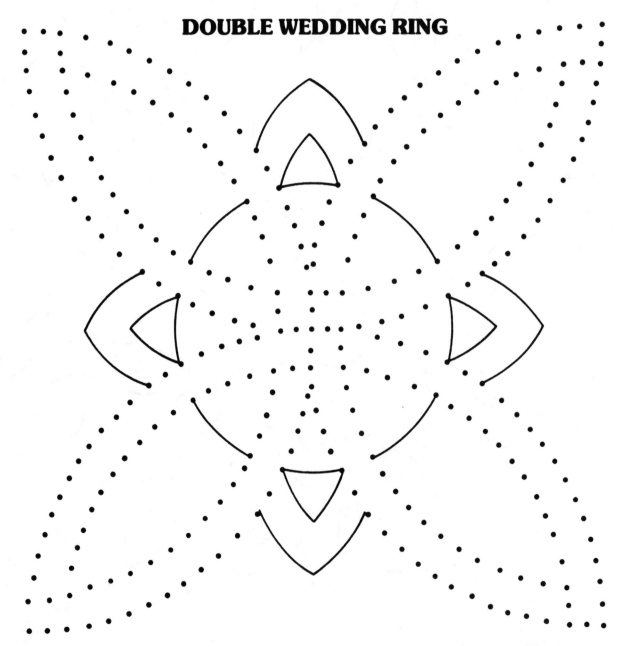

FEATHER CIRCLE

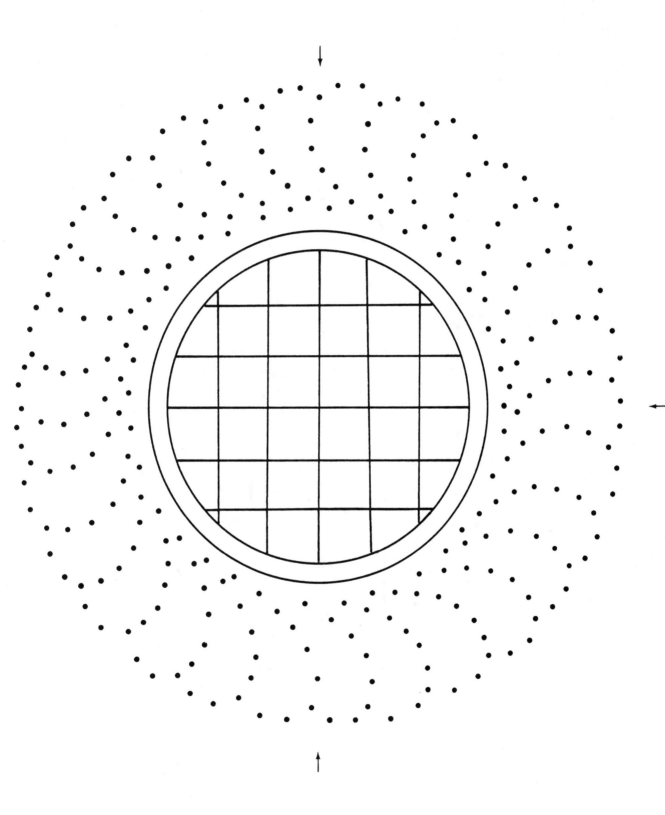

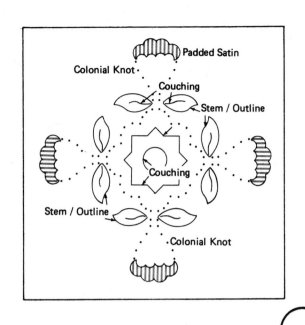

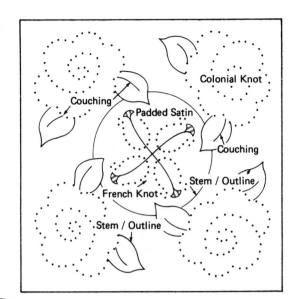

ROSE OF SHARON

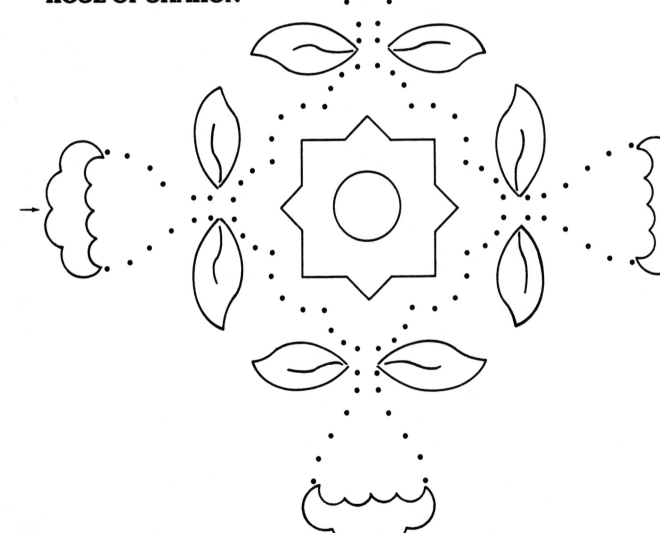

ROSES AND TULIPS

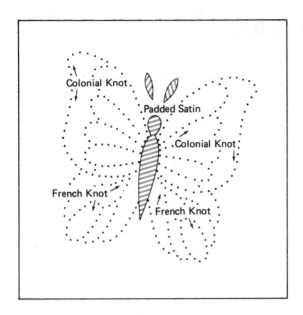

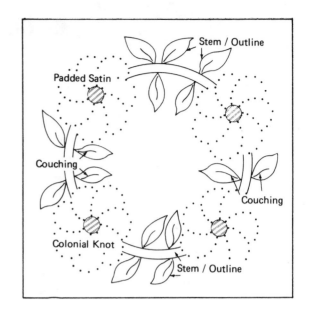

BUTTERFLY

PRESIDENT'S WREATH

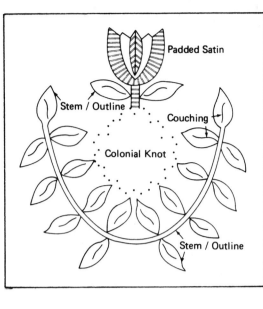

PRAIRIE FLOWER

ROSE AND FAN

Stem / Outline

Colonial Knot

Couching

Stem / Outline

Padded Satin

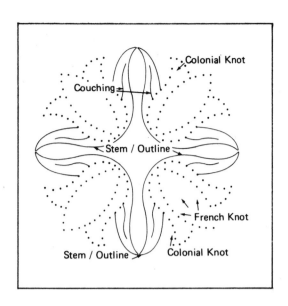

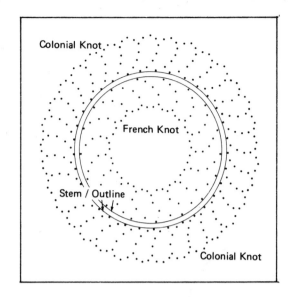

TULIPS

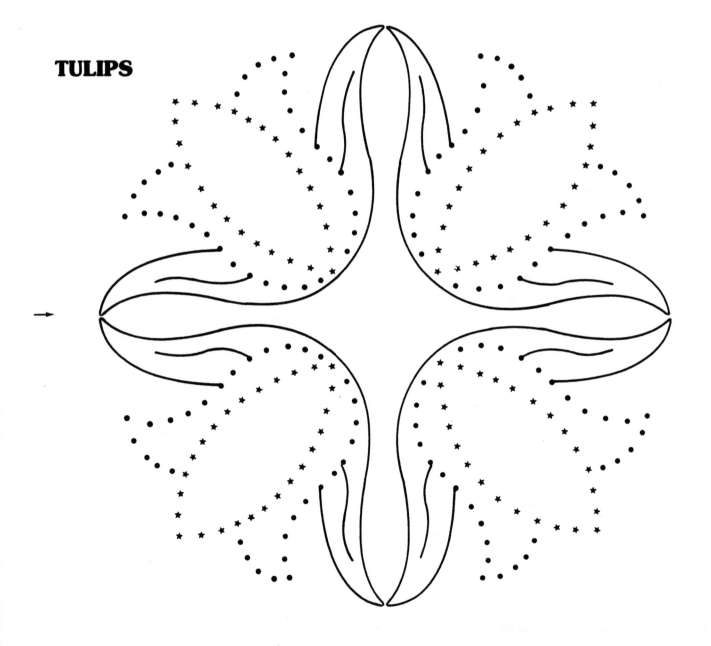

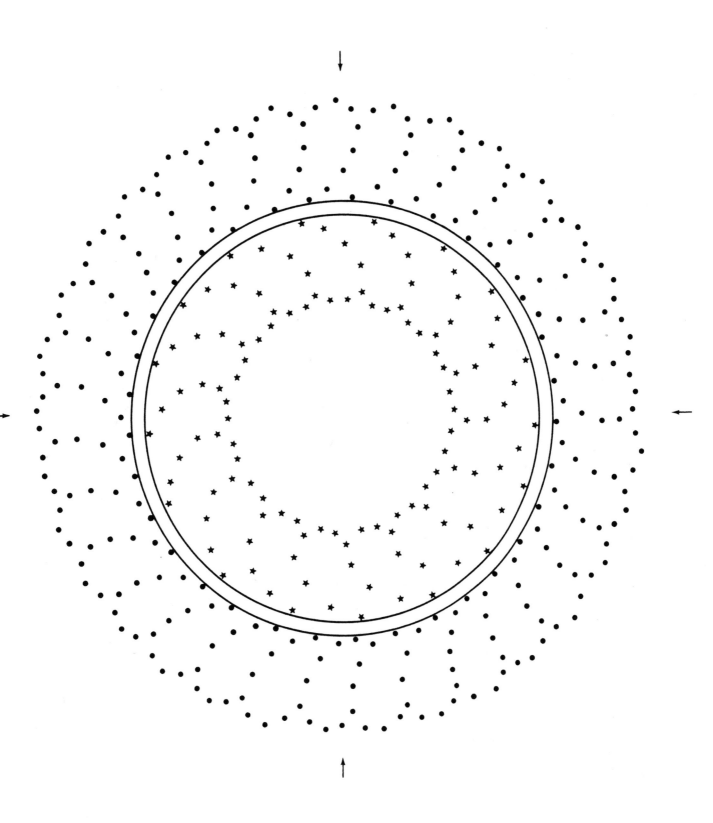

ROSE

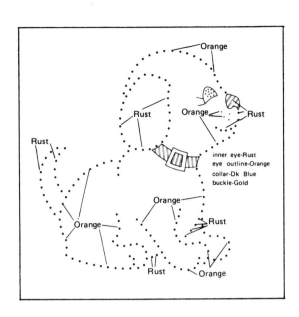

DOGGY

STITCH KEY
- • = Colonial Knot
- · = French Knot
- —— = Stem/Outline
- ▥ = Satin Stitch

CLOWN

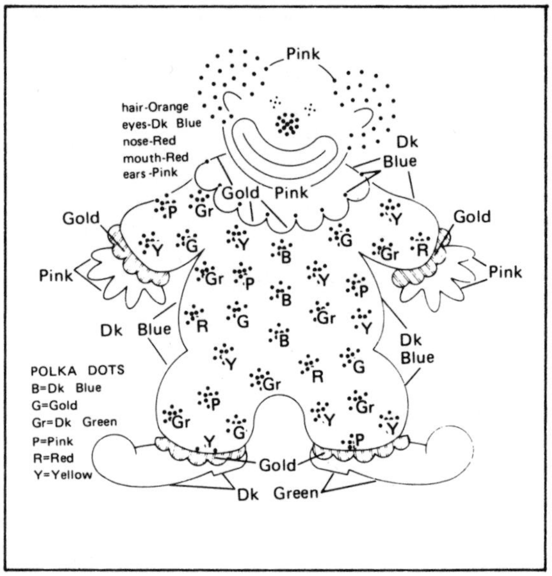

hair-Orange
eyes-Dk Blue
nose-Red
mouth-Red
ears -Pink

Pink

Dk Blue

Gold   Pink

Gold   Gold

Pink   Pink

Dk Blue   Dk Blue

POLKA DOTS
B=Dk Blue
G=Gold
Gr=Dk Green
P=Pink
R=Red
Y=Yellow

Gold

Dk Green

TEDDY

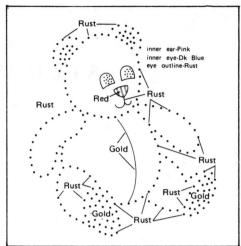

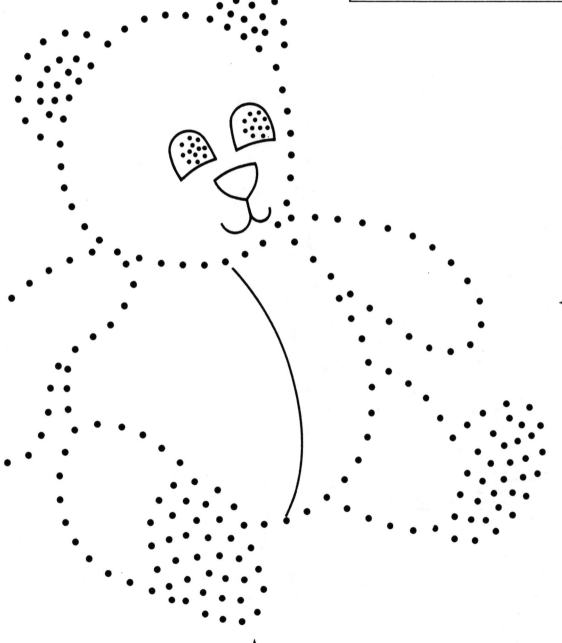

SAILBOAT

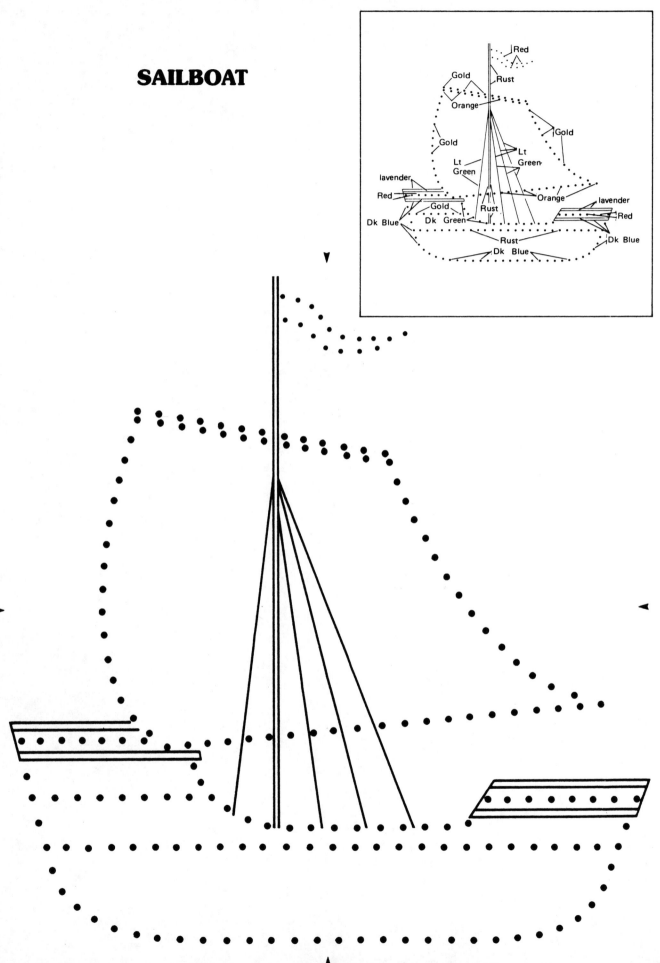

MERRY-GO-ROUND

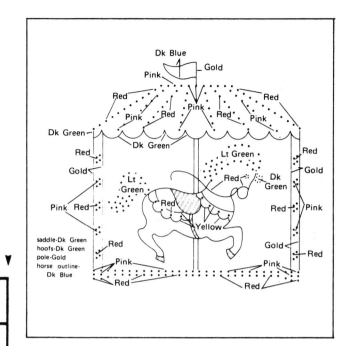

Dk Blue
Gold
Pink
Red
Red
Pink
Red
Pink
Red
Red
Pink
Dk Green
Dk Green
Red
Lt Green
Red
Gold
Lt Green
Red
Dk Green
Red
Pink Red
Red
Pink
Yellow
Gold
saddle-Dk Green
hoofs-Dk Green
pole-Gold
horse outline-
Dk Blue
Red
Pink
Red
Pink
Red
Red

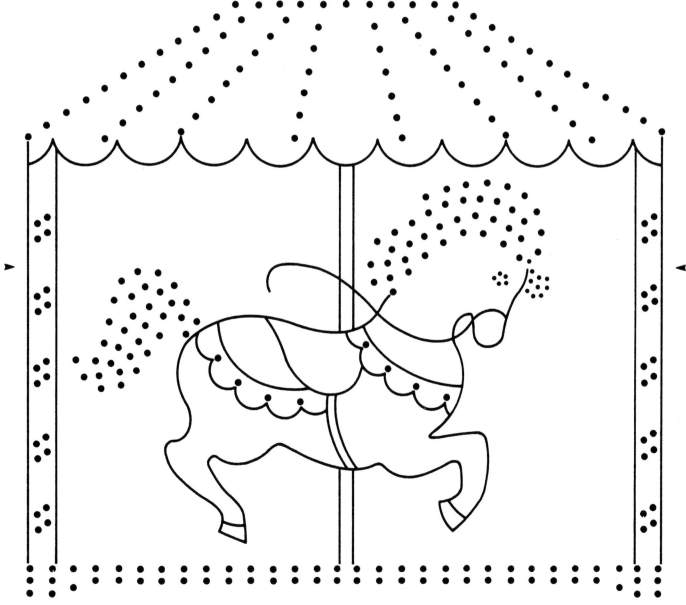

CHOO-CHOO

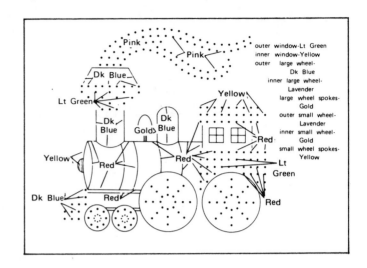

DOLLY

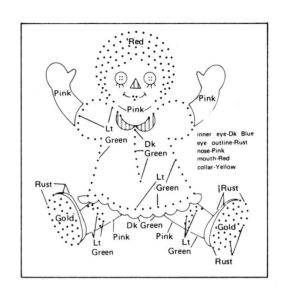

HUMPTY-DUMPTY

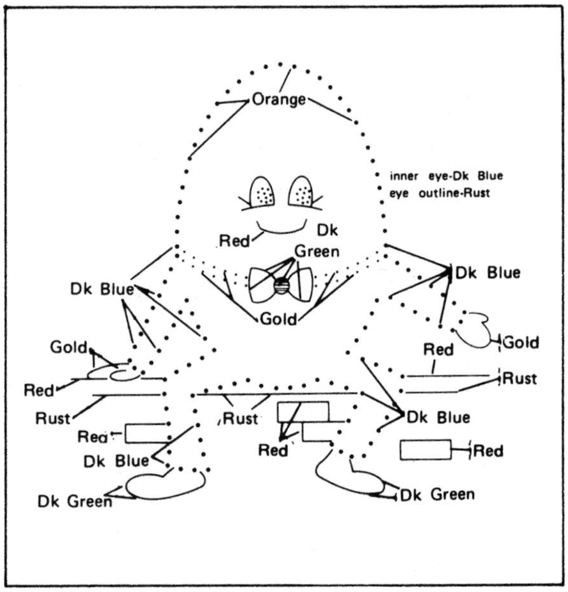

Orange

inner eye-Dk Blue
eye outline-Rust

Red

Dk Green

Gold

Dk Blue

Dk Blue

Gold

Red

Red

Rust

Rust

Rust

Red

Dk Blue

Red

Dk Blue

Dk Green

Dk Green

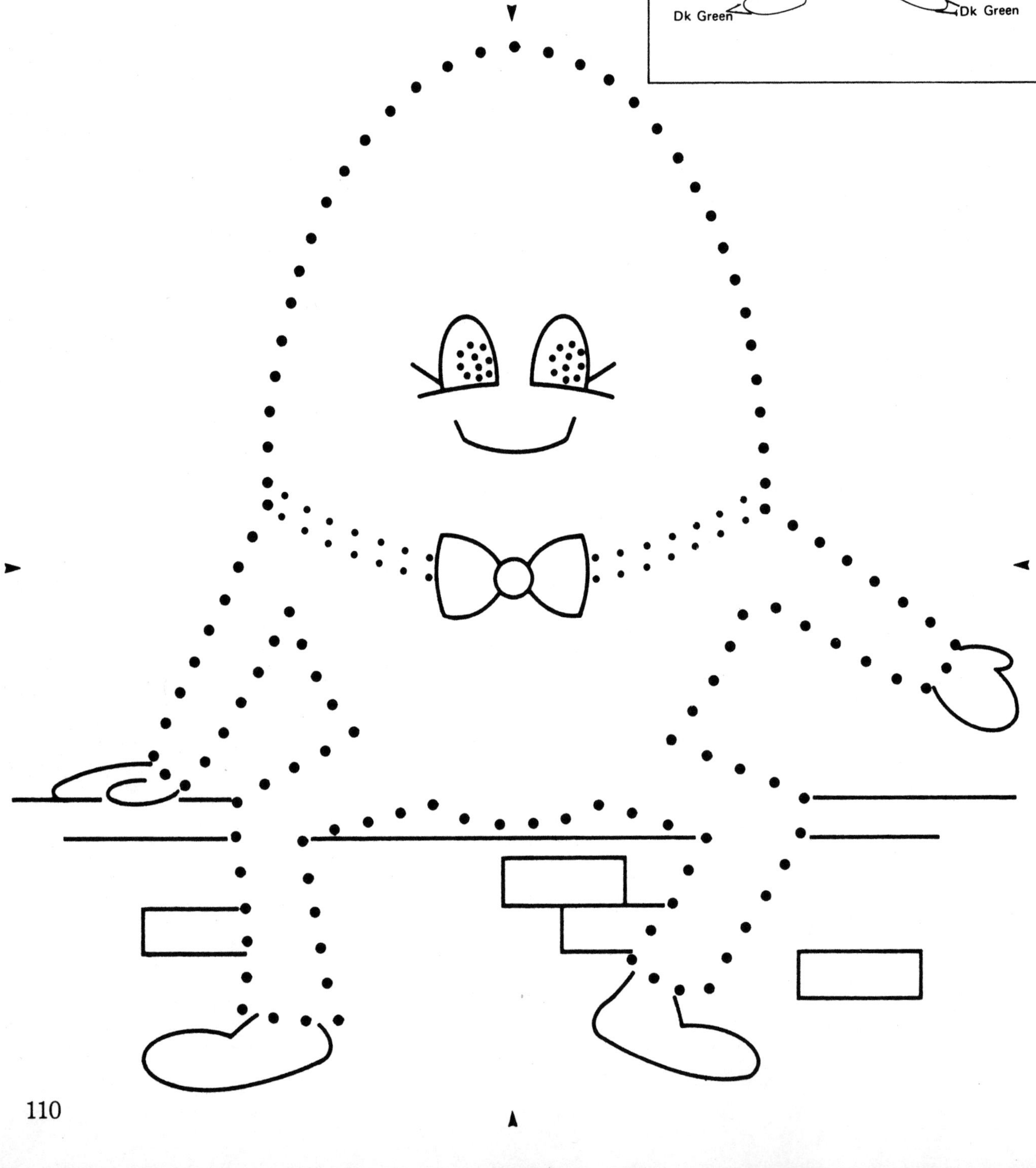

KITTY

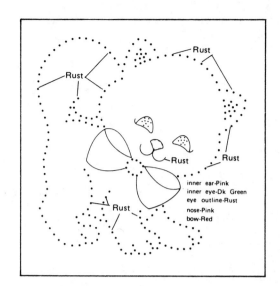

inner ear-Pink
inner eye-Dk Green
eye outline-Rust
nose-Pink
bow-Red

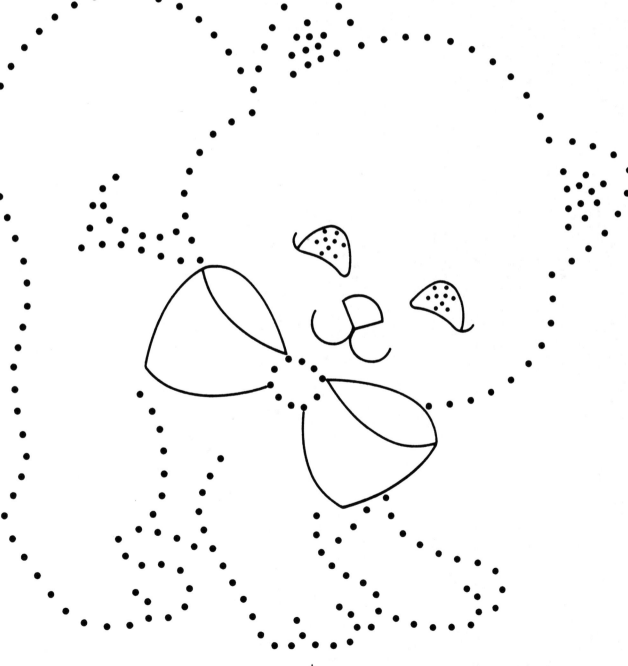

LAMBY

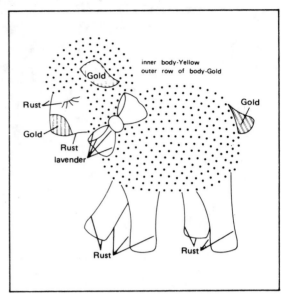

inner body-Yellow
outer row of body-Gold

Gold

Rust
Gold

Rust
lavender

Gold

Rust   Rust

112

BUNNY

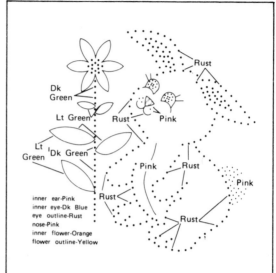

inner ear-Pink
inner eye-Dk Blue
eye outline-Rust
nose-Pink
inner flower-Orange
flower outline-Yellow

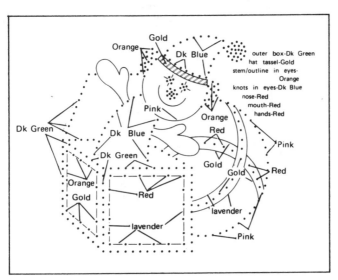

JACK-IN-THE-BOX

CANDLEWICK SUNBONNET SUE QUILT

Sunbonnet Sue has long been a favorite of quiltmakers, and here she appears in a new guise—as a delightful Candlewick crib quilt. If you don't have a baby who would just love to snuggle under this quilt, then turn Sunbonnet Sue into a beautiful wall hanging.

Size:

Approx 36″ × 47″

Materials and Equipment

All fabric requirements are based on 44″–45″ wide material. If you are using narrower fabric, adjust yardage accordingly. 1⅔ yards unbleached muslin (*for blocks*)
(*NOTE: Use a good quality 100% cotton which has not been preshrunk.*)
1 yd natural-color cotton (*for sashing, borders and binding*)
1½ yds fabric (*for backing*)
1 package crib-size quilt batting
175 yds natural Candlewicking thread
Fabric shears and embroidery scissors
Sewing, Candlewicking and quilting needles
Sewing and quilting thread (*white is preferred*)
Beeswax

Embroidery hoop
Quilting hoop
Straight pins
Iron
Thimble
Tissue or tracing paper
Water-soluble marking pen

Before cutting, wash and iron fabrics to be used for framing, borders, binding and backing. **Do not prewash fabric to be used for Candlewick blocks**. Make sure that the grain of all fabric is straight.

Instructions

Step 1: Cut a piece of Candlewick fabric 14″ × 14″ for each block. Follow instructions on page 87 and trace designs.

Step 2: Candlewick the blocks.

Step 3: Following instructions on page 87, wash blocks in cold and hot water.

Step 4: Following instructions for blocking on page 5, block each quilt block to a perfect 8½″ square. Cut your cardboard template with an 8½″ square opening.

Step 5: There is no framing around the blocks in this quilt. From sashing fabric, cut nine sashing strips 3½″ wide by 8½″ long.

NOTE: Be sure the top of each block is in the right position.

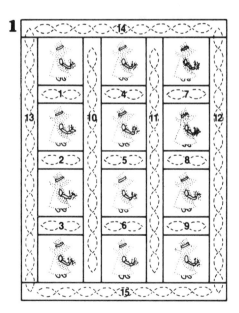

Place a sashing strip (**Fig 1: No. 1**) across the bottom of one block right sides together and stitch. Then sew same piece of sashing to top of another block. In the same manner stitch second sashing strip (**Fig 1: No. 2**) to bottom of second block and then to top of third block. Join third sashing strip (**Fig 1: No. 3**) to bottom of third block and top of fourth block. You have a vertical strip of four joined blocks. Following **Fig 1** for placement, make two more vertical strips in same manner. You now have three vertical strips each measuring 41½" (which includes ¼" seam allowance at top and bottom). Press all seams to one side—not open—before joining next seam. Cut two sashing strips, each 3½" wide and 41½" long. Sew one strip to each side of center row of blocks (**Fig 1: Nos. 10 and 11**). Sew first and third rows of blocks to these same strips, being sure that tops and bottoms of all blocks line up exactly. Press seams.

Step 6: Now complete quilt by adding borders to top, bottom and sides. Cut four border strips, each 3½" wide. Cut two 41½" long and two 36½" long. In same manner as for vertical sashing, sew two longer border strips to right and left sides of quilt top (**Fig 1: Nos. 12 and 13**). Then sew shorter border strips to top and bottom (**Fig 1: Nos. 14 and 15**). Give quilt top final steaming, making sure all corners are square and all seams pressed to one side.

Step 7: Quilt or tie top and attach binding following directions on page 6.

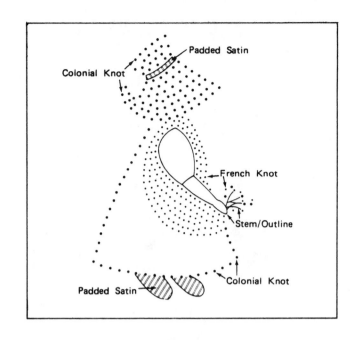

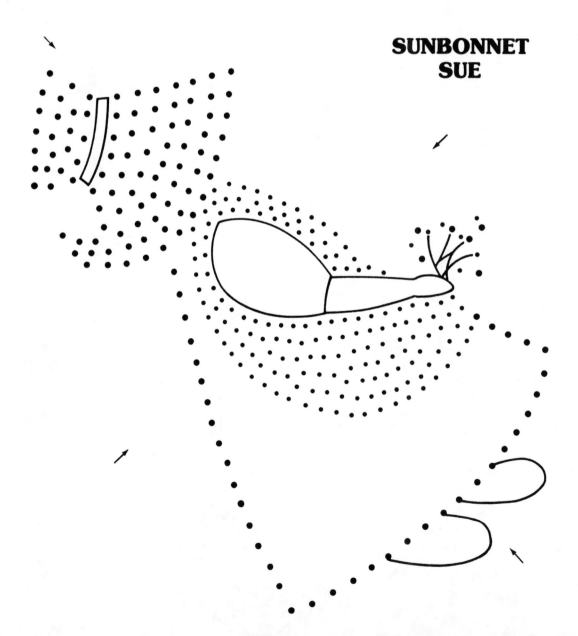

SUNBONNET SUE

Lace Net

It's fun! It's easy! It's fast! It's the new "old" skill of Lace Net embroidery.

If you have ever followed a cross stitch or needlepoint chart, you will find Lace Net embroidery charts simple and easy to complete. As you work, you will see the form take shape—as if by magic—on a blank piece of net. And soon you will discover that you have created a piece of lace—perfect for today's decorating scene.

Modern Lace Net embroidery was developed during the Victorian era of great needlework. It was an attempt to imitate the beautiful lace (called *Opus Filatorium, Punto a Maglia, Lacis* or *Spiderwork*) created in the convents of Europe during the middle ages.

Some people refer to this craft as Lace Net Darning. That's a terrible name for such a delightful craft. Darning was something we used to do with socks. Save the "darning" for when you make mistakes. Then as you correct your errors, you can say as many "darns" as you want.

LACE NET HOW-TO

THE FABRICS

Years ago, fabric used for lace net embroidery was made by hand in a process known appropriately as "netting". Today this fabric is machine made in both ecru and white and is available at your local needlework or craft store or department.

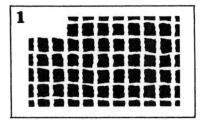

The net, woven with six meshes to the inch, is made of a smooth poly/cotton and is easy to work with. The meshes are perfectly square, but vertical threads (those parallel to the selvage) are usually slightly thicker than horizontal threads (**Fig 1**). If you work with thicker threads as the verticals, the work will be smoother as the thinner (horizontal) threads will be "lost" in the weaving. Which thread used as the vertical is a matter of personal preference, but in a large project—such as our quilts—make sure that the thicker threads are always running in the same direction.

THE THREADS

Special threads made of 100% mercerized cotton are now available for Lace Net embroidery. The #5 size is used for the Darning stitch which has been used to make our quilt blocks.

In addition #5 Pearl Cotton, 6 strands of embroidery floss, candlewicking thread, or darning thread could be used for the quilt blocks.

The traditional colors for Lace Net embroidery are ecru on ecru fabric and white on white fabric.

THE NEEDLES

Use a needle with a blunt point and a long eye such as a #18 tapestry needle. Specially packaged "Lace Net Assortments" are also now available.

HOOP AND FRAMES

When Lace Net embroidery was worked on hand-made netting, the work was done in a frame. Today—with machine-made net—use of a hoop is optional though preferable. Since it is important that you work evenly without pulling too tightly, we find it easier to work with a hoop. When stretching the net in the hoop, leave a little "give" in the fabric.

LACE NET EMBROIDERY CHARTS

As in other forms of counted embroidery—such as counted cross stitch—charted designs are the key to Lace Net embroidery. It is the chart that shows you just which squares of the net are to be stitched. Each square on the chart equals one hole of the net. The lines equal the bars which surround the hole. The squares which are to be worked are printed in a gray tone (▓). You will fill each square with several journeys of the thread.

Charts can be foolers in one sense: The size of the charted design is not necessarily the size that your finished work will be. The worked size is determined by the number of meshes per inch of the mesh you select. For example, most of our designs are 72 meshes × 72 meshes. When you work this on the lace net (6 meshes to the inch) the finished design will be 12″ × 12″, which is somewhat larger than the chart in the book.

THE STITCHES

The stitch used to create the patterns in our quilt blocks is the traditional Darning or weaving stitch (**Fig 2**). The technical name for this stitch is "Reprise" or "Point de Reprise".

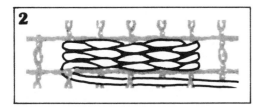

The stitch can be worked horizontally (**Fig 3**) or vertically (**Fig 4**). You can work an entire design either horizontally or vertically; or you can work both horizontally and vertically in the same design, giving a pleasing change of light and shade to the work. We do not recommend your trying this technique until you have had some experience working one way. All of the designs shown in our book were worked horizontally.

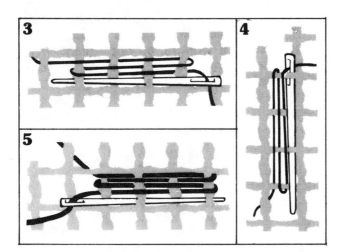

In Darning Stitch, each pass of the needle takes the thread over one bar of net and under the next; the process is reversed in row beneath, making the thread pass over those bars which it previously passed under until a closely woven section is completed (**Fig 5**).

Step 1: Thread needle with one 36″ strand #5 thread. Do not knot.

Step 2: Starting from back at A in **Fig 6**, and leaving a 3″ tail, bring thread over and under bars. At end of row, go around bar (B) and bring needle back in opposite direction going under bars you worked over on the row above and vice versa.

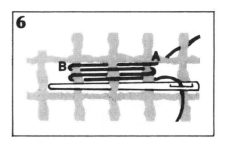

Step 3: Weave back and forth across as many squares as are indicated on the chart. The squares must be packed with thread so that when work is finished, it will give the impression of a piece of lace. We used five or six rows of #5 thread in our quilt blocks.

Step 4: When the thread gets too short, finish it off by running needle neatly across back through some of the just completed stitches; trim thread close to back of work. It is a good idea to finish a row before ending your thread rather than stopping in the middle of a row. Now rethread the tail you left in step 2 and run the thread behind the completed embroidery. Thread your needle with another 36″ length of thread. Either secure by weaving through backs of several stitches or by leaving a tail which can be rethreaded and finished off as described above. Continue working your pattern.

Step 5: The work should look the same on front as back. Therefore, if you wish to skip squares, you can hide thread through the back of darning threads. If you cannot hide threads because the jump across unfilled squares is too large, simply finish the row as in step 4 by running thread through back of work. Clip thread close to work and start to work again as in step 1.

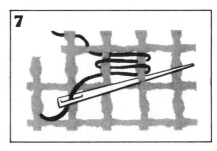

Step 6: The same rule of working over and under bars applies even when working on one square. Work back and forth across square as in (**Fig 7**), going around the bars on each side, working over and under.

SPECIAL HINTS

1. There is no special place to start. You may work from left to right or from right to left (a boon for left-handed stitchers). You may work from top down or from bottom up.

2. Keep your tension even. Do not pull your threads so tightly that you distort the bars.

3. To keep your work smooth, "rake" stitches with your needle as you work rows.

WORKING THE LACE NET

The designs for the quilt blocks used in making the quilts appear on pages 121 to 132 and 134 to 136. Each chart has arrows along side and bottom. Extend these arrows, and where they meet is center of design.

Find center of net by folding in half horizontally and vertically. Mark center with basting threads, in both directions, that cross at center. These markings are pulled out later. Use this center square as starting point for counting. It does not matter where you begin stitching, but it is probably easier to begin at top of design. Matching centers of fabric and chart, count upwards to top of design and start stitching.

When embroidery has been completed, measure worked area. Depending upon amount of stitching and your tension, embroidery will probably have shrunk somewhat in size. In addition, it may shrink more in one direction than the other, making it no longer square. The size does not matter that much, but the embroidery should be a perfect square—especially when making the quilt. Therefore, you will need to block your work.

Wet embroidery (if soiled, wash carefully in lukewarm water and mild suds) and place face down on ironing board. Pull edges of embroidery straight with your fingers. Making sure that work is perfectly square, place pins at corners and at several places along edges to hold in place. Cover embroidery with damp cloth and steam with warm iron (or use steam iron). *Never let iron rest on stitches; let steam do the work!*

LACE NET SAMPLER QUILT

What could be lovelier than to use authentic old-time quilt designs to create a magnificent Lace Net quilt. If the making of an entire quilt looms as too large a project, why not try a block as a pillow, a doily, or a wall hanging. In the photograph, we show sections of our quilt used to make smaller projects.

Size

55″ × 72″

Materials

1⅞ yds Lace Net (60″ wide) *or* twelve 16″ squares Lace Net (*see note below*)
3½ yds 44″-wide cotton fabric (*for blocks, sashing, borders and binding*)
4½ yds 44″-wide cotton fabric (*for backing*)
1 package twin-size quilt batting
900 yds Lace Net thread.

NOTE: Although each finished quilt block will be a 14″ square, we recommend working on a 16″ square of Lace Net. This extra material will allow for error when centering design. If you are extremely careful, you can work with a 15″ square of Lace Net for each block.

Before cutting cotton, wash and iron fabric. Make sure that grain of fabric is straight.

NOTE: Our quilt, pictured here makes up into a comforter for a twin bed. If you prefer a larger covering suitable for a double bed, make 20 Lace Net blocks by repeating 8 of your favorites. Then set blocks 4 across and 5 down. This will make a quilt measuring 80″ × 89″. Material requirements for this quilt are:
2¾ yds Lace Net or twenty 16″ squares Lace Net
10 yds 44″-wide cotton fabric
1 package double bed-size quilt batting
1400 yds Lace Net thread.

Instructions

Step 1: Stitch Lace Net designs on page 121 to 132 making sure design is centered on fabric. Wash and block each Lace Net block according to above instructions. Be certain that each block is a perfect square.

119

Step 2: From your cotton fabric, cut twelve 14½" squares, and center a Lace Net embroidery piece on each square. An easy way to do this is to find center of your embroidery again and to locate center of cotton block (fold in half horizontally and vertically). Match both centers. Baste Lace Net embroidery to cotton block. Start in center and sew toward edge with large basting stitches in diagonal lines. Permanently attach embroidery to block by sewing all around edge of block along ¼" seam allowance. Re-move basting stitches. When you have finished sewing Lace Net to cotton block, trim any excess Lace Net extending beyond edge of quilt block. Now work with Lace Net embroidery and fabric block as one.

Step 3: There is no framing around the blocks in this quilt. Look at *Fig 1* for arrangement of blocks. From cotton fabric, cut nine sashing strips 3½" wide × 14½" long. Place sashing strip (*Fig 1: No. 1*) across bottom of "Lemoyne Star" block right sides together and stitch. Then sew same piece of sashing to top of "Basket" block. In same manner stitch second sashing strip (*Fig 1: No. 2*) to bottom of "Basket" block and then top of "Blazing Star" block. Join third sashing strip (*Fig 1: No. 3*) to bottom of "Blazing Star" block and to top of "Bridal Wreath" block. You now have a vertical strip of four joined blocks. Following *Fig 1* for placement, make two more vertical strips in same manner. You now have three vertical strips each measuring about 65½" (which includes ¼" seam allowances at top and bottom). Press all seams to one side before joining next seam. Cut two sashing strips each 3½" wide and 65½" long (or length of your strip of blocks). Sew one strip to each side of center row of blocks (*Fig 1: Nos. 10 and 11*). Sew first and third row of blocks to these same strips, being sure that tops and bottoms of all blocks line up exactly. Press seams to one side—not open.

Step 4: Now complete quilt top by adding borders to top, bottom and sides. Cut four border strips, each 3½" wide. Cut two 65½" long (or length of your quilt top) and two 54½" long (or width of your quilt top). In same manner as for vertical sashing, sew two longer border strips to right and left sides of quilt top (*Fig 1: Nos. 12 and 13*). Then sew shorter border strips to top and bottom (*Fig 1: Nos. 14 and 15*). Give quilt top final steaming, making sure all corners are square and that all seams are pressed to one side.

Step 5: Quilt or tie top and attach binding following directions on page 6.

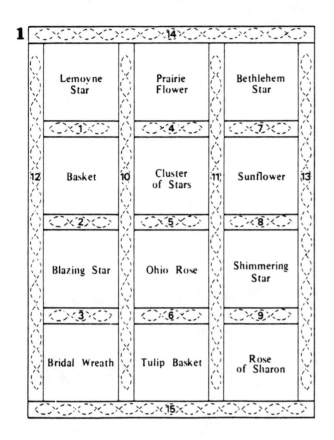

LEMOYNE STAR

72 meshes × 72 meshes

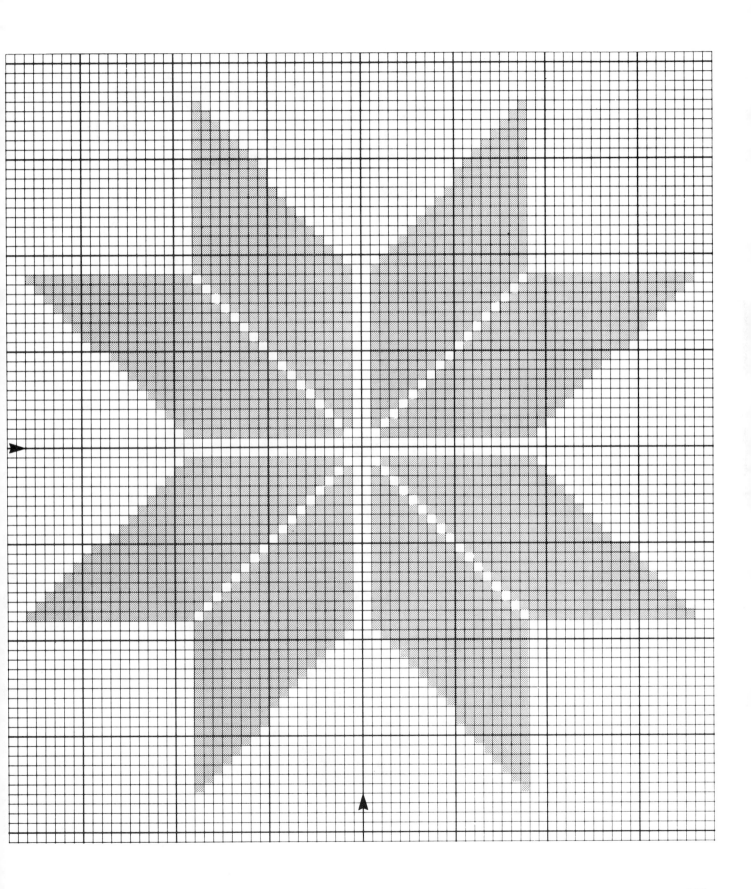

TULIP BASKET
72 meshes × 72 meshes

BRIDAL WREATH
72 meshes × 72 meshes

SHIMMERING STAR

72 meshes × 72 meshes

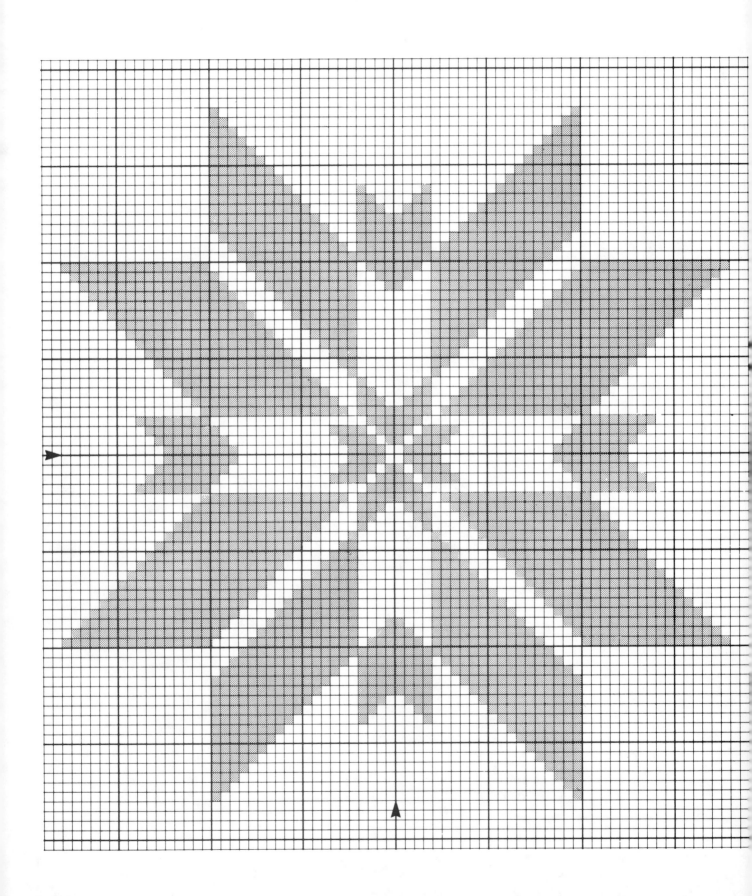

OHIO ROSE

72 meshes × 76 meshes

BLAZING STAR
72 meshes × 72 meshes

SUNFLOWER
72 meshes × 72 meshes

CLUSTER OF STARS
72 meshes × 72 meshes

BASKET

72 meshes × 72 meshes

BETHLEHEM STAR
72 meshes × 72 meshes

PRAIRIE FLOWER
71 meshes × 66 meshes

ROSE OF SHARON
76 meshes × 76 meshes

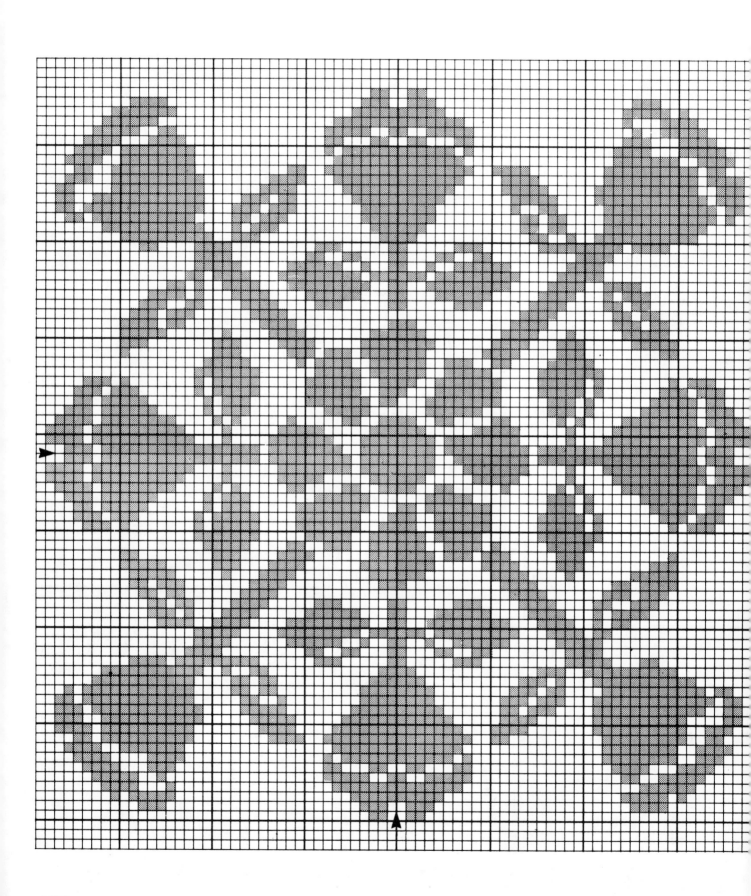

LACE NET CRIB QUILT

What a charming gift for a new mother: an old-fashioned Lace Net crib quilt for the new-born baby! No need to worry whether the baby will be a boy or a girl; these charming motifs will delight either. And while you're working, why not make some adorable pillows with one or two of the blocks?

Size

Approx 36″ × 47″

Materials

1 yd Lace Net (60″ wide) *or* twelve 10″ × 10″ pieces Lace Net
1½ yds 44″-wide cotton fabric (*for blocks, sashing, borders, binding*)
1⅓ yds 44″-wide cotton fabric (*for backing*)
140 yds Lace Net thread
1 package crib size quilt batting

Instructions

Step 1: Stitch twelve Lace Net designs on pages 134 to 136. Wash and block each design according to above instructions, making sure that blocks are square.

Step 2: From cotton fabric, cut twelve 8½″ squares. Center Lace Net embroidery on each square. An easy way to do this is to find centers of embroidery and cotton block (fold in half horizontally and vertically). Match both centers. Carefully baste Lace Net embroidery to cotton block. Start in center and sew toward edge with large basting stitches in a number of diagonal lines. Permanently attach

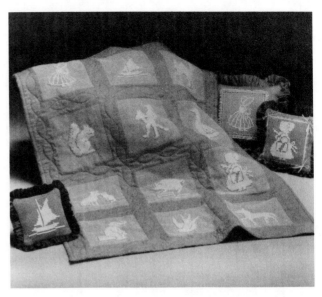

Lace Net to block by sewing all around edge of block along ¼″ seam allowance. Remove basting stitches. Trim any excess Lace Net extending beyound edge of quilt block. Work with Lace Net embroidery and fabric block as one.

Step 3: There is no framing around the blocks in this quilt. Cut nine sashing strips 3½″ wide × 8½″ long. Making sure top of each design is in right position, place sashing strip (***Fig 1: No. 1***) across bottom of "Sunbonnet Sue" block right sides together and stitch. Then sew same piece of sashing to top of "Sylvester Squirrel" block. In same manner stitch second sashing strip (***Fig 1: No. 2***) to bottom of "Sylvester Squirrel" block and the top of "Donald Dog and Cathy Cat" block. Join third sashing strip (***Fig 1: No. 3***) to bottom of "Donald Dog and Cathy Cat" block and top of "Emma Elephant" block. You now have a vertical strip of four joined blocks. Following ***Fig 1*** for placement, make two more vertical strips in same manner. You now have three vertical strips each measuring 41½″ (which includes ¼″ seam allowance at top and bottom). Press all seams to one side—not open—before joining next seam. Cut two sashing strips, each 3½″ wide and 41½″ long. Sew one strip to each side of center row of blocks (***Fig 1: Nos. 10 and 11***). Sew first and third rows of blocks to these same strips being sure that tops and bottoms of all blocks line up exactly. Press seams.

Step 4: Complete quilt by adding borders to top, bottom and sides. Cut four border strips, each 3½″ wide. Cut two 41½″ long and two 36½″ long. In same manner as for vertical sashing, sew two longer border strips to right and left sides of quilt top (***Fig 1: Nos. 12 and 13***). Then sew shorter border strips to top and bottom (***Fig 1: Nos. 14 and 15***). Give quilt top final steaming, making sure all corners are square and all seams pressed to one side.

Step 5: Quilt or tie top and attach binding following directions on page 6.

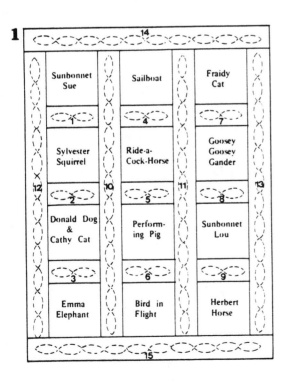

1

Sunbonnet Sue	Sailboat	Fraidy Cat
1	**4**	**7**
Sylvester Squirrel	Ride-a-Cock-Horse	Goosey Goosey Gander
2	**5**	**8**
Donald Dog & Cathy Cat	Performing Pig	Sunbonnet Lou
3	**6**	**9**
Emma Elephant	Bird in Flight	Herbert Horse

14

12 10 11 13

15

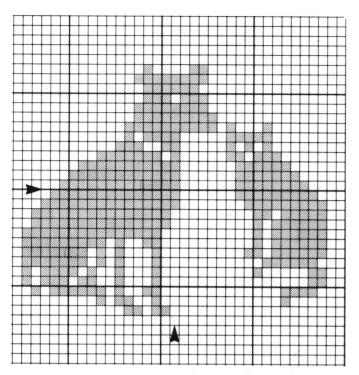

DONALD DOG AND CATHY CAT
33 meshes × 26 meshes

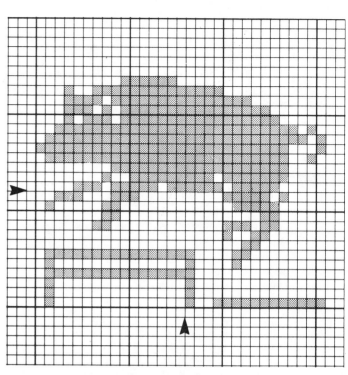

PERFORMING PIG
31 meshes × 24 meshes

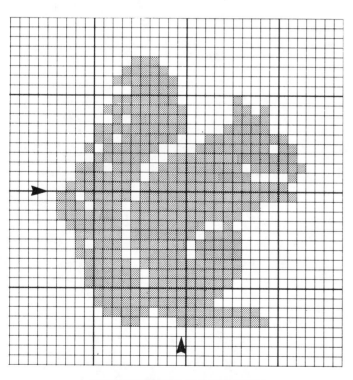

SYLVESTER SQUIRREL
27 meshes × 28 meshes

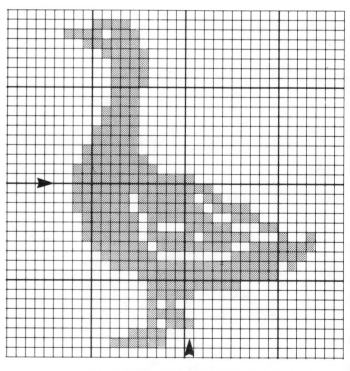

GOOSEY-GOOSEY-GANDER
27 meshes × 34 meshes

134

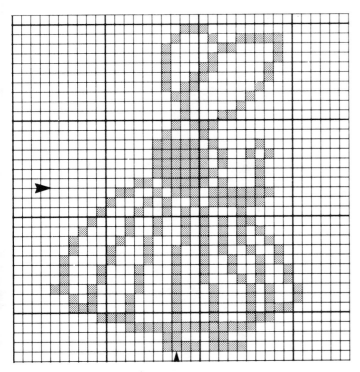

SUNBONNET SUE
27 meshes × 34 meshes

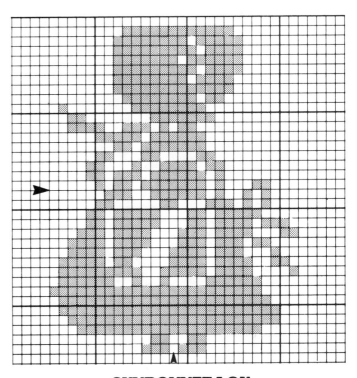

SUNBONNET LOU
27 meshes × 34 meshes

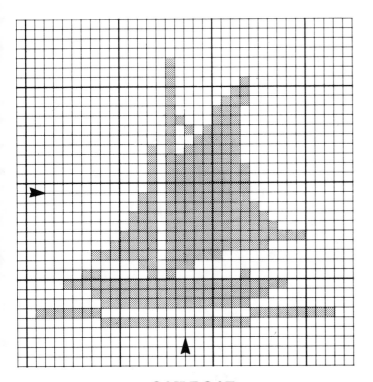

SAILBOAT
32 meshes × 28 meshes

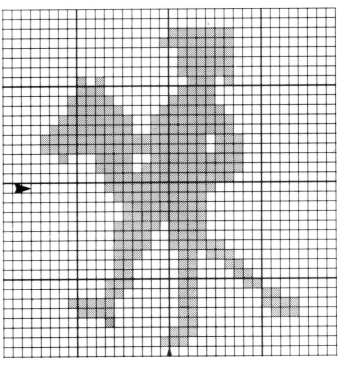

RIDE-A-COCK-HORSE
28 meshes × 33 meshes

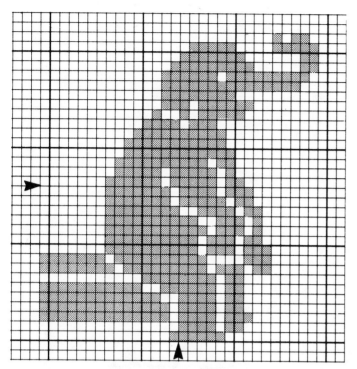

EMMA ELEPHANT
30 meshes × 32 meshes

FRAIDY CAT
29 meshes × 32 meshes

HERBERT HORSE
33 meshes × 30 meshes

FLYING BIRD
28 meshes × 31 meshes

Sewing Machine Quilts

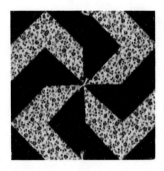

If the only craft you ever practice is sometimes sewing up a seam on a sewing machine, then you too can make a wonderful quilt. Take out your sewing machine, oil it up, dust it off, and follow our step-by-step illustrated instructions, and before you know it, you'll be creating family heirlooms.

SEWING MACHINE QUILTING HOW-TO

TEMPLATES

All of the pattern pieces used to make the sewing machine quilts are given in actual-size templates printed on page 143. Each quilt will indicate which templates are used for that quilt. Carefully trace the template shapes onto heavy cardboard, such as medium-weight illustration board, and cut them out. (Special plastic for making templates is also available in quilt shops or departments.) It is important that all templates be cut out carefully because if they are not accurate the patchwork will not fit together. Use a pair of good-size sharp scissors (not the scissors that you will use to cut your fabric, of course), a single-edged razor blade or an X-Acto knife. Be careful not to bend corners of triangles.

CUTTING THE PIECES

Some quilters prefer to mark and cut all pieces for an entire quilt before beginning. Others prefer cutting and piecing a block at a time. We enjoy a compromise between the two. Cutting out 168 triangles can be monotonous, but there are moments when you may relish the rhythm of doing the same thing over and over. Why not cut and piece four blocks; then cut and piece the next four. **Whatever method you choose, cut and piece a trial block first**. This will give you a chance to double-check the pattern and to make certain that you like both design and color.

Each of the sewing machine quilts requires 42 blocks. The illustrated step-by-step instructions for construction (pp. 140–142) will give you the number of pieces necessary for one block and total number of pieces necessary for entire quilt. Make your trial block and then decide how you want to cut and piece the remainder of the quilt.

Start by laying your laundered, freshly-ironed fabric on a smooth surface with wrong side up. Have all your supplies ready: scissors, rulers, sharp pencils, marking tools, templates, etc. Check cutting instructions for your quilt.

Lay cardboard template on the wrong side of the fabric near top left edge of material (but not on selvage), placing it so that as many straight sides of piece as possible are parallel to crosswise and lengthwise grain of fabric (*Fig 1*).

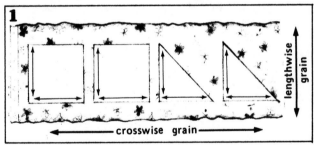

Try to keep long side of triangles on true bias by placing short sides of triangles on straight of fabric. Trace around template. You can mark with a regular well-sharpened, hard lead pencil (using a light color for dark fabrics and a regular pencil for light fabrics), but there are some quilt makers who like to use fabric marking pens, tailor's chalk—even architects' pencils (intended for writing on blue prints). Test any marking material to make certain that it will not run when wet. There are a number of cold water-soluble quilt marking pens currently on the market. These pens can be used to mark both back and front of fabric so you can use them later for marking your quilting design. Cold water supposedly makes these markings disappear, but once again never trust manufacturers' labels. Always test everything just to be sure. Hold your pencil or marker at an angle so that the point is against the side of the template.

Continue moving template and tracing it on fabric required number of times, moving from left to right and always keeping straight lines parallel with grain. You will save fabric if you have pieces share a common cutting line as in *Fig 2*, but if this is confusing, leave a narrow border or margin around each piece. Use a sharp scissors and cut accurately.

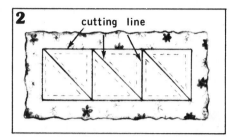

SEWING THE QUILT TOP

Now for the fun part: sewing the pieces together on the sewing machine! Machine piecing is done with the straight stitch foot and throat plate on the machine. Set your machine for about 10 stitches to the inch.

The traditional seam allowance in quilting is ¼″ so you are going to need some method to make sure that you sew with a perfect ¼″ seam. If your machine has the ¼″ marked on the throat plate, you are in luck. If not, measure ¼″ from your needle hole to right side of the presser foot and place a piece of tape on plate. Keep edge of your piece lined up with this marking, and you will be able to sew a perfect ¼″ seam.

Now let's assume that you are making the sample block for the "Flyfoot" quilt as described on page 140.

Step 1: Our illustrated step-by-step instructions tell us that we are to join 16 light triangles and 16 dark triangles to make 16 squares. So let's place two triangles together with right sides facing. Make certain that edges of both pieces are even (*Fig 3*). Pin triangles together. Do this for all sixteen sets of triangles. (Be careful that you do not sew over pins even if your machine permits this. Sewing over pins weakens seams.)

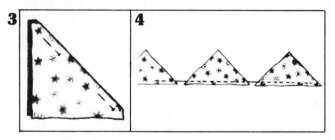

Construct 16 blocks using the production line method. In this method you do not begin and end your thread with each patch, but you let the thread run over a continuous row (*Fig 4*).

Feed pieces through the machine as in *Fig 5* and stop when you have made 16 squares.

Snip squares apart (*Fig 6*). Don't worry about threads coming undone. They will eventually be anchored by the cross seams.

After you have joined two pieces together, press seams flat to one side, not open. Now on to step 2.

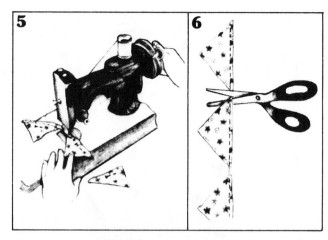

Step 2: Our illustrated step-by-step instructions tell us to join squares made in Step 1 into two different strips. Place two squares together, noting carefully how squares are to be turned. Pin squares together (*Fig 7*). Now feed squares through sewing machine, stopping when you have made 4 strips (*Fig 8*). Iron seams flat. Repeat process for the second strip, making 4 more strips.

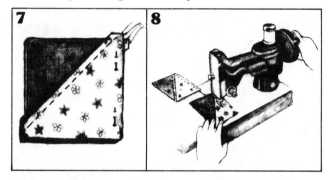

Step 3: Our illustrated step-by-step instructions tell us to join strips made in Step 2. Again carefully note how strips are to be turned. Pin. Feed through sewing machine to make four blocks.

Step 4: Carefully following diagram in illustrated step-by-step instructions join the squares made in step 3 to make the quilt block.

Iron all seams flat. You might want to turn seam on top in one direction and seam on bottom in opposite direction.

You have made one complete block. Wasn't that fun!

HINT: As you sew, be careful of fabric's tendency to stretch. This is especially true along bias edges, such as long sides of triangles. Sewing machines are not infallible. Some constantly fight to stretch top fabric. You can learn to win! You may be forced to ease top fabric while stretching bottom fabric on some seams. It helps if you try to feed fabric through the machine with grain straight at all times. Be especially careful of stretching bias seam allowances. Whenever possible, sew from large end to pointed end of a piece, and always iron in direction of grain.

BLOCKING THE BLOCKS

Place completed block on ironing board and pull edges straight with your fingers. Cover block with damp cloth and steam with warm iron (or use steam iron). Iron block perfectly flat with no puckers. Do edges first; center last. Move iron as little as possible to keep block from stretching. Blocks should be perfect 12½″ squares. (The finished block will actually be a 12″ square; the extra ¼″ all around being seam allowance that will be used when joining blocks.) Blocks which are slightly larger or smaller can be blocked into shape. Draw a perfect 12½″ block on a piece of paper and place on ironing board. Pin block in place on paper pattern and steam press in place following above instructions.

JOINING THE BLOCKS

Join blocks to make seven rows of six blocks each. Use ¼″ seam allowance at all times, and press seams to one side. Be extremely careful that all blocks are turned in right direction. When horizontal rows are completed, join two rows together, matching seam lines. Then add next rows. Press seams to side.

HINT: When crossing seams, be especially careful to match seam to seam. One learns to do this fairly accurately while sewing by feeling with fingers. It helps if the lower seam is turned one way and the top seam the other, so press seams for odd numbered rows in one direction; even numbered rows in the other.

ADDING BORDERS

Now complete quilt by adding borders to top, bottom and sides. (The illustrated step-by-step instructions give suggestions for border fabric.) Cut four border strips, each 3½″ wide. Cut two 84½″ wide (or length of quilt top) and two 78½″ wide (or width of quilt top plus side borders).

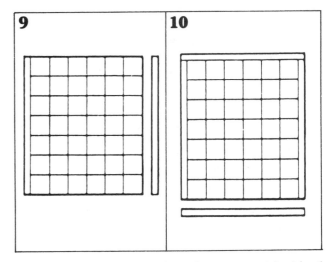

Right sides together, attach one long strip to right side of quilt and one to left (**Fig 9**). In same manner, sew shorter border strips to top and bottom (**Fig 10**). Use ¼″ seam allowance.

Give quilt top a final blocking, making sure all corners are square and all seams are pressed to one side. (If you find it difficult to work on ironing board now, you might try your dining room table or living room floor.)

FINISHING THE QUILT

Quilt or tie top and attach binding following directions on page 6.

FLYFOOT SEWING MACHINE QUILT

This delightful quilt is quite easy to make! It's made up entirely of triangles that are joined together in an interesting pattern. The quilt in the photograph has been tied instead of quilted; that makes it even easier! Just follow our illustrated step-by-step instructions, making sure that you turn the squares correctly.

Size of quilt top
78″ × 90″

Size of quilt block
12″

Construction
Set 6 across and 7 down with 3″ border all around

Materials and Equipment
5¼ yds dark fabric (*for patchwork*)
6¼ yds light fabric (*for patchwork, borders, binding*)
5½ yds fabric (*for backing*)
82″ × 94″ sheet polyester quilt batting
1 pair fabric shears (*for cutting fabric*)
cardboard or plastic (*for templates*)
1 pair sharp scissors, single-edged razor blade or X-Acto knife (*for cutting templates*)

Sewing thread
quilting thread
beeswax
thimble
straight pins
sewing needles

sewing machine
quilting needles
quilting hoop or frame
marking pencils
yarn (*for tying*)

Instructions

 dark

 light

Using template, cut the following:

FOR ONE BLOCK	FOR QUILT
16 dark	672 dark
16 light	672 light

Step 1:
Make 16 for block
Make 672 for quilt

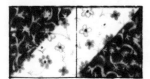

Step 2:
Make 4 for block
Make 168 for quilt

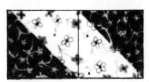

Make 4 for block
Make 168 for quilt

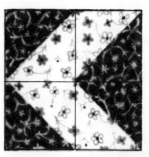

Step 3: Join strips made in Step 2.
Make 4 for block
Make 168 for quilt

Step 4:
Join squares made in Step 3.
Make 1 for block
Make 42 for quilt

Finish quilt, following directions on pages 6 and 139, using light fabric for borders and binding.

CARD TRICKS SEWING MACHINE QUILT

Take two triangles—one big and one small—and put them together in an ingenious manner, and you have the secret to old-time quilt making. This quilt is a perfect example of that technique. And made with our step-by-step illustrated instructions, this quilt is also easy to make. Amaze your friends and relatives with your very own "card tricks".

Size of quilt top
78″ × 90″

Size of quilt block
12″

Construction
Set 6 across and 7 down with 3″ border all around

Materials and Equipment:
2 yds brown print (*for patchwork*)
2 yds rust (*for patchwork*)
2 yds rust print (*for patchwork*)
¾ yd beige (*for patchwork*)
3 yds blue (*for patchwork, borders, binding*)
5½ yds fabric (*for backing*)
82″ × 94″ sheet polyester quilt batting
1 pair fabric shears (*for cutting fabric*)
cardboard or plastic (*for templates*)
1 pair sharp scissors
single-edged razor blade or X-Acto knife (*for cutting templates*)

Sewing thread	sewing needles	marking pencils
quilting thread	sewing machine	yarn (*for tying*)
beeswax	quilting needles	
thimble	quilting hoop or	
straight pins	frame	

Instructions

 brown   rust   beige

rust print   blue

Cut the following:

TEMPLATE	FOR ONE QUILT	FOR BLOCK
A	2 brown	84 brown
A	2 rust	84 rust
A	2 rust print	84 rust print
A	2 blue	84 blue
A	4 beige	168 beige
B	2 brown	84 brown
B	2 rust	84 rust
B	2 rust print	84 rust print
B	2 blue	84 blue
B	4 beige	168 beige

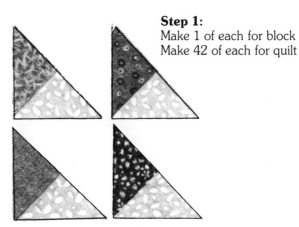

Step 1:
Make 1 of each for block
Make 42 of each for quilt

Step 2: Join triangles made in Step 1 to A triangle.
Make 1 of each for block
Make 42 of each for quilt

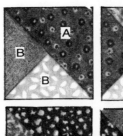

Step 3:
Make 1 of each for block
Make 42 of each for quilt

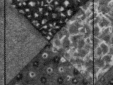 

Step 7: Join Steps 2 and 4.
Make 1 for block
Make 42 for quilt

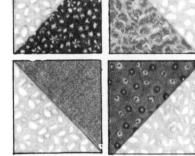

Step 4: Join triangles made in Step 3.
Make 1 for block
Make 42 for quilt

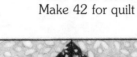

Step 5:
Make 1 of each for block
Make 42 of each for quilt

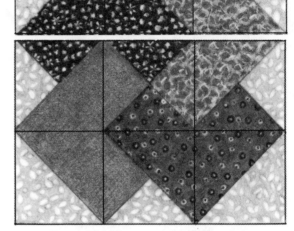

Step 8: Join strips made in Steps 6 and 7.
Make 1 for block
Make 42 for quilt

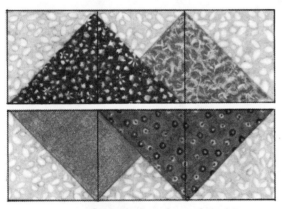

Step 6: Join Steps 2 and 5.
Make 1 of each for block
Make 42 of each for quilt

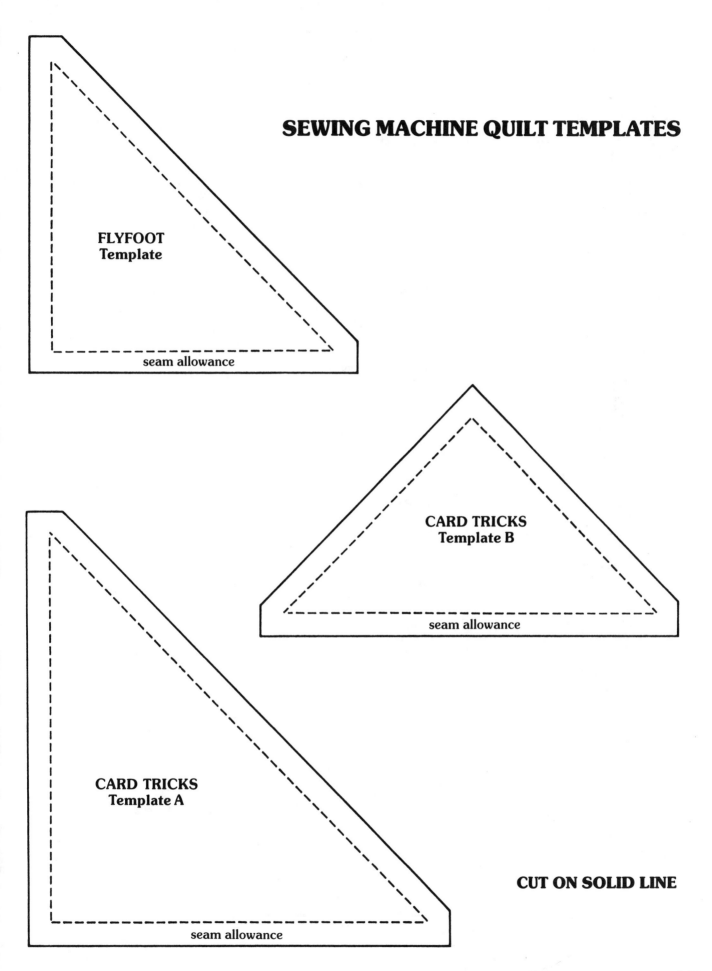

SEWING MACHINE QUILT TEMPLATES

FLYFOOT
Template

seam allowance

CARD TRICKS
Template B

seam allowance

CARD TRICKS
Template A

seam allowance

CUT ON SOLID LINE

Index